Trust and Power
Taking Care of Ourselves through Drama

Penny Casdagli

Jessica Kingsley Publishers
London and Philadelphia

First published in the United Kingdom in 1999 by
Jessica Kingsley Publishers Ltd
116 Pentonville Road
London N1 9JB, England
and
1900 Frost Road, Suite 101
Bristol PA 19007, USA.

www.jkp.com

Copyright © 1999 Penny Casdagli

Library of Congress Cataloging in Publication Data
A CIP catalogue record for this book is available from the Library of Congress

British Library Cataloguing in Publication Data
Casdagli, Penny
Trust and power: taking care of ourselves through drama
1.Psychodrama 2.Drama – Therapeutic use
I.Title
618.9'2'891523

ISBN 1 85302 556 9

Printed and Bound in Great Britain by
Athenaeum Press, Gateshead, Tyne and Wear

Contents

For Tony Newton –
actor, colleague and friend
(18 March 1962 – 13 September 1995)

Foreword

How to Build a Ship

You gather people and plant in them
love of and longing for the wide
vast endless sea.
You do not gather people
and tell them to collect wood,
draw up a plan,
and build a ship.

Antoine de Saint-Exupéry

As an art therapist who has worked and continues to work with people who have suffered abuse, I find Saint-Exupéry's statement a succinct yet profound description of my experience as an advocate. Therapy through creativity centres on advocating a person's belief in his or her own life-affirming energy. The act of creating, in any medium, enables the individual to become acquainted with abilities and strengths he or she may not have known they had. Although the creative process is a painful one, it fosters the ability to face life with courage and vitality.

Those who have undergone such a process can often themselves be advocates for others. Penny Casdagli's workshops are an example of how this process sustains and perpetuates itself, as participants find the trust and power to take care of themselves and perhaps, in the future, to advocate a similar process for others.

Once given the real tools for building a ship – love and passion for life – the voyage can begin.

Offra Kamar
Jerusalem, 1998

CHAPTER 1

Introduction

Theatre and drama have long been recognised as the most effective vehicle for health and safety education. To be able to cause change, to move and to inform audiences makes this area one of the most innovative and rewarding for any theatre practitioner. I first became involved in making theatre with and for young people in 1975, and although still very much involved with mainstream theatre, I have never stopped being fascinated by the scope and energy of this work, which speaks as powerfully to the adults in its audience as to young people and children. Indeed, I have spent over 20 years devising multifaceted projects, many of which have been performed in different languages simultaneously by fully integrated companies of performers that evidence a lively Equal Opportunities policy. These projects have included plays, workshops, training programmes, seminars, publications and videos, all of which have been part of an imperative to try to push back the boundaries of access and to offer excellent professional theatre for change. Amongst the issues I have explored in depth are bullying and grief, and I have been fortunate in having colleagues as passionate about this kind of theatre as those agencies that have commissioned and funded it.

In 1990, I was approached by a group of social workers and psychologists from a central London borough with a very low referral rate of children and young people at risk. They asked if I would be interested in writing a play about sexual abuse for audiences of young children. The notion was to see if such a play, to be performed just once in a local school, would help the problem. I declined. To produce a play for a single performance would be extremely expensive, and writing a play about child abuse for primary school children seemed to me a negative and unnecessarily complex approach, and one fraught with hazard.

Instead, I suggested a series of interactive drama workshops for groups of eight to ten year olds exploring trust and power, themes which embrace many important aspects of taking care of ourselves and others. The workshops, facilitated by a small team of three working closely with the teachers and carers of the participants, would use puppets as well as games and exercises, traditional material, stories, plays and discussion and would be designed and executed with special reference to the different languages and cultures of those taking part. After detailed discussion on all our parts, the authority commissioned the workshops.

From my own knowledge of abuse issues, I knew it was crucial that a firm distinction was always drawn between fact and fiction, between imagination and information, and between speculation and experience. This is where the puppets would come in. By their being used to tell the stories and act out the plays of the workshops, they would provide the perfect device for carrying the narrative only, creating a valuable distance for both facilitators and participants to reflect on the stories so they could be discussed more freely which, it was hoped, would enhance self-esteem by improving communication.

As we edged towards committing ourselves and our skills to the project, now named the Trust and Power Workshops, I arranged professional supervision for the team I had assembled, a senior social worker, extremely experienced in the whole area of child abuse. With her, we worked through our initial fears and worries so that we could draw on our own experience and use it safely. Encouraging and informative, she talked to us about child protection and child abuse from the Social Services' point of view and also in regard to the law. She told us that abuse included physical, mental, verbal and emotional abuse as well as sexual abuse, and that neglect and adults making children responsible for their emotional welfare were also more subtle and less recognised forms of abuse.

We looked at the effects of abuse of all kinds on children and young people and learnt that when a child is abused their self-esteem can be seriously reduced and that:

- they can become less confident in themselves and less communicative
- self-esteem is the most consistent psychometric indicator of future achievement in school
- an abused child can internalise a fear of failing which leads them to avoid taking risks at all costs
- not asking questions, not making mistakes, not attempting new tasks, not asking for help, even not getting too close to people, poor concentration and disruptive behaviour can result.

Other effects of abuse on children include: not being able to take care of themselves and not being able to take responsibility for themselves or their part in a situation; sleeplessness; hatred of mistakes both those made by others and by themselves; gains of weight to hide within or loss of weight to become invisible; a neglect of self sometimes expressed in low and destructive self-esteem or by substituting the needs of others and caring for them as the expense of oneself; rigidity; and lack of confidence about change; feelings of isolation; loss of innocence and being old beyond their chronological years; personality changes; memory impairment; not being able to play; craving attention; abhorring attention; emotional numbness; physical clumsiness; not being able to visualise the future; self-harm; and eating disorders were all effects of abuse that could last into adulthood. Several adult survivors of abuse shared with us their memories of school, which we could add to and compare with our own experiences. It was generally agreed that the findings supported the view that many abusers were abused as children, and their children are more likely to become abusers themselves.

Supervision was available for all of us during the workshops themselves and immediately afterward which helped us as a group and as individuals to debrief and evaluate the project and its impact on ourselves.

Almost a year passed between the first approach and the actual start of the workshops which gave everyone enough time to prepare, reflect on and evolve our plans as well as get to know each other better. Nothing like this had ever been done before, and it was good to be able to talk and question so freely.

Meanwhile I entered a period of intensive research developing the materials and the content of the six Trust and Power Workshops. This included asking the help and advice of specialists in special needs and child protection work, reading widely, and interviewing people who were very different from each other, but who had in common first-hand experience of the challenges which negative circumstances can make on self-esteem, and who were all willing for their contribution to be used in whatever way seemed best for the workshops.

During this period, whilst attending an anti-bullying conference, I heard an educational psychologist remark that wherever there was 'good self-esteem, there was no bullying'. I also remembered John Hall of ChildLine telling me that in a sense every call to ChildLine was one of bereavement, mourning a loss of innocence. I linked that to the knowledge I had from my work on grief that a bereavement reduces self-esteem. I thought about these three insights a great deal, although I did not understand fully the relationship they had with each other at the time, nor how closely they interact. I borrowed Elizabeth Kübler Ross' affecting metaphor of grief being a journey with seven different stages and made the workshops into a journey in six parts, starting with trust, then power, body, feelings, communicating, and finally, learning; a journey, destination unknown, whose sole purpose was what would be learnt on the journey itself. Going on a journey always represents some sort of risk, acting with courage in leaving one place for another, perhaps unknown, not knowing what will happen to us while we travel. In other words, I reached for a situation in which all we have is ourselves, where we need a map and to know how to take care of ourselves, and in which we can come to understand that we can only really take good care of ourselves if we take care of each other. I made this the workshop structure.

A school was chosen and a timetable drawn up of the six Trust And Power Workshops to be done with the whole of Year Four, 120 eight- to ten-year-olds. Each of the six workshops would be repeated with four class groups over a period of three weeks with two weeks' preparation and a week in which to debrief and evaluate. The school had a high intake of refugee children and children with no English, with a significant minority of the school community always changing and being moved on as their families looked for accommodation. Many had fled their own countries because of war. The theme of journeys would be a vivid reality for them. The workshops were to be presented in English, British Sign Language and Bengali, and while many other languages existed in that group, the reality of multilingualism is that any language starts to open up in terms of comprehension when other languages and forms of communication are valued and juxtaposed.

A detailed curriculum, given later in this book, was developed outlining the knowledge, skills and attitudes each workshop needed to cover. Since that original curriculum was written, the workshops have evolved, changed and been modified by the groups and the facilitators who created them. Although some of the curriculum learning goals are no longer dealt with in the workshops, and other points have been developed with objectives of their own, it still forms an indispensable blueprint or map and is constantly referred to whenever these workshops are undertaken.

Three areas in the project proposal were seen by all of us as being of paramount importance and which we knew had to be incorporated into the process of the workshops. These were self-esteem, taking learning risks and relationship skills with peers and adults. From the abstract points that formed the curriculum, much time was spent considering how to translate those points into:

1. exercises in which the teaching points could be experienced

2. puppet plays

3. true stories to illustrate each session's themes.

Something else borne in mind in devising the curriculum of the workshops was that the very exercises designed to promote protection, self-protection, responsibility and self-esteem might also act as indicators in the case of children for whom these were in short supply.

Four simple puppets, Red, Blue, Green and Blue, as well as a dragon and an elephant were commissioned from the designer, Barbara Cowdery. Her first attempts were conventional, yet once she let herself be as creative as a child, the final puppets had a beautiful, raw, child-like power. It was very important that the puppets should be simple but unique, as they were going to be the 'identity figures' and act as an empathetic medium between us, the facilitators and them, the participants. Through reading Alice Miller's *Thou Shalt Not Be Aware* (1991), I realised that the use of puppets was also striking illustration of her perception that when abuse takes place, the abuser robs the abused of feeling the centre or subject of his or her own life and treats him or her like an object. The puppets were objects that could be animated to act out stories and plays based on real life, in which shifts and changes in the dynamics of trust and power and self-esteem could be analysed and solutions to dilemmas discussed and rehearsed.

More and more I felt that self-esteem was emerging as the critical factor in the whole project, and that if any benefits or healing that took place due to the workshops resulted in a restoration of playfulness and spontaneity, theatre and drama were going to be likely catalysts. Self-esteem therefore became the most important concept in the planning of the workshops, and with it the speculation that for any true notions and practice of both trust and power to be understood and for the participants to feel safe and empowered, it would happen through enhanced self-esteem.

We were aware before we started in the school that several of the children we were to work with were already at risk, and for some boundaries had already been compromised. We wanted to create an environment in which anything could be discussed with no hidden agendas. I also felt it to be crucial that, through working carefully with our supervisor, we were able to own all the stories. In other words, by being able to use and contribute our own stories of, for example, times in our lives when our trust had been broken, we were living models of the fact that we can survive our difficult experiences and – more important – know what use to make of them. We had chosen to speak personally. I think everyone involved respected that.

The puppets evolved themselves as we developed the sessions. First, they could speak to us, and we could tell their stories as adult narrators. Then, when we held them, and spoke of them and for them, we were their advocates – this choice of word is again greatly influenced by Alice Miller and her writings. She describes lucidly the difference between advocacy and pedagogy in *For Your Own Good* (1988). This distinction informed how we held the puppets when they were the vehicles of our stories. When they make their first appearance, they are held like babes in arm, and whisper silently in their narrator advocates' ears. They then become ourselves and other protagonists in the stories and plays, and then finally, the facilitators bobbed out of sight, they become their own puppet selves, Yellow, Green, Blue and Red, leaving behind the mythical dragon and anthropomorphic elephant.

The workshops led to a full length play, *Shabbash!* which toured nationally in the UK and which has been performed in Hungary, Bangladesh and Singapore. It was an incredibly difficult play to write, and one that I could only have written with the help of my Yellow, or advocate at that time, the art therapist Ofra Kamar, whose client I was. A phenomenon of working on self-esteem is that it tends to disappear as soon as you start. An advocate, defined here as 'someone who is on your side and who will speak for you if you want them to', is necessary. He or she is someone who is outside your process and yet can accompany you in it, and someone who can say to you when you stumble, as I so often did, 'So you fell down. So you can get up!'

The changes that happen in the participants are evidence of the value of listening and being listened to, and are and were perhaps the most profound effect of the project. I have facilitated the workshops in widely differing organisations, as well as in schools, and go on learning from the participants and being moved by their contributions. Each time the workshops have taken place, they have been monitored and evaluated. The results all point to the effectiveness of this kind of work. I hope this book will encourage others to use theatre and drama in the area of self-esteem and protection issues and that it will prove a helpful contribution.

Finally, I would like to express my thanks to all the many children and adults who have helped and advised me in the development of these workshops, stories and plays, including special thanks to Betty, to Christopher, Dorothea and Wendy Casdagli, John Hall of ChildLine, Claudia, Neil Dawson, Anna Fairtlough, Iona Fletcher, Francis Gobey, Dietrich, David Gillespie, Kezia Jo Halliday, Karen Gui, all at Hallfield Junior School, Hallgrave Park School and Blue Gate Fields School, Robbie Jones, Marcia, Ofra Kamar, Komal Kandhari, Margaret Kennedy, Judith Lowe, Ian Lucas, Marianne March, Brenda McHugh, Mina Mokid, Tony Newton, Jean Nicholas, Selene O'Kane, Lucy Pitman-Wallace, Mo Ross, Angela Sims, Karen Smith, Rena Sodhi, Hannah Thompson, and particularly to Gwen Williamson for her invaluable support throughout the writing of this book.

CHAPTER 2

The Trust and Power Workshops

The theme of these Trust and Power workshops is taking care of ourselves. Taking care of ourselves involves protection, responsibility, self-esteem, relationship, community and control. This sequence or journey of interactive workshops has been especially designed, executed, monitored and evaluated to give its participants a direct experience, often independent of language, of these aspects of taking care of ourselves.

The Trust and Power workshops are a sequence of six interactive drama workshops of one-and-a-quarter hour's duration each. Although each session can be used on its own, as can any part of a session, together they form a journey with six stages, the themes of which are trust, power, body, feelings, communicating, and learning. Developed after intensive research into the issues of child protection, personal safety and self-esteem, these workshops have now taken place in many schools and other organisations, both in the United Kingdom and abroad. Evolved over a period of seven years, they are presented here for use by, certainly, teachers of personal, social and health education, but also by health promotion workers, social or residential workers, playleaders, therapists, carers, survivors of child abuse, and all those concerned with protection issues and self-esteem at all ages. The rationale behind the use of all the elements in the workshops is explained with its description along with the full text of all the workshop stories and plays together with a choice of alternative stories. Originally designed for primary school students between the ages of eight to ten, and to be used with many languages, the workshops can easily be adapted to other age and special needs groups, including those using wheel chairs.

These workshops can and do change their participants, and, by definition, their facilitators. Any change brings with it a departure from the known, the loss of which is sustainable in this case because something else can be arrived at, something new, something which has been disguised or hidden and which is waiting to be revealed freshly and safely for each person that participates. For this reason, the workshops are in the form of a metaphysical journey.

The Trust and Power workshops are a journey towards, and an examination of, the positive goals of enhancing self-esteem by developing the capacity to learn through taking risks and improving relationship skills. The sequence has been especially designed to set up a positive movement (or virtuous circle) of connections between themes, while at the same time acknowledging and valuing the negative movement or vicious circle which any form of abuse can instigate and, by holding these two forces in a balanced tension, to provide a space in which the potential for resolution and learning can be realised.

In their sequential order, the themes of the workshops are trust, power, body, feelings, communicating, and learning. In creative circumstances a child *trusts* their carers, and is *empowered* by that trust; they then feel safe in their *body*, which then becomes a reliable source of *feelings* which can be listened to and *communicated* to others when necessary. All of which gives a secure basis for *learning* – especially learning from 'mistakes' or bad experiences, which are unavoidable in any life. However, when a person, particularly a young person or child, is abused in any way or in any circumstance, their trust is broken, which immediately disempowers them – perhaps making it difficult for them to trust others, peers or adults. Their body is hurt – by words, blows, neglect or by their boundaries being violated, which includes sexual abuse – but in a context where feelings normal to hurts of the body are disallowed; and so their feelings become confused and even suspect, making the communicating of them, along with other ways of relating, difficult. All of which sets up blocks to learning, by replacing trust and self-confidence with fear and low self-esteem.

The workshops are fun, of course, otherwise they wouldn't be valuable. Few facilitators will need reassuring that participants learn most when they enjoy themselves at the same time. Rooted in our lives and concerns, the most important aim is to equip the younger participant in particular with the means of protection before he or she needs it, and to create resources to fall back upon if and when that is necessary in the future. Amongst the issues dealt with to achieve this aim is how to discover what we can learn from what has happened to us in the past, and how to prepare for a future; the recovery from bad experiences; self-protection and a strengthening of identity and confidence; improved communications between groups and individuals, and how to value the richness of difference, particularly as manifest in cultural difference and language.

Within the practical execution of the workshops there are a range of particular aims which the workshop design intends to realise, among which are: listening with an increasing span of attention to others; asking and responding to questions and commenting on what has been said; being confident in using one's own first language; the ability to work in pairs and groups; distinguishing between 'positive' and 'negative' messages; interpreting experience; problem solving through critical reflection, hypothesising, predicting, and providing alternative solutions; acquiring and improving drama skills such as mime and assuming roles and working within them; and the ability to reflect on process, content and the participant's own contribution to that.

About the workshops

Each workshop uses exercises, games, movement, sound, puppet plays and stories, drawing and discussion to examine the positive and negative aspects of its respective theme and how it relates to the whole area of trust and power. The choice and timing of these exercises has been carefully decided to allow each exercise to develop and resonate one upon the other. In *Trust*, for instance, the workshop has the implicit expectation that all participants can and do have the potential for trusting, and provides appropriate circumstances in which the group can consider and experiment with trust whilst simultaneously building trust with each other and their facilitators. Conversely, it also assumes that most participants have had or will have experiences of their trust being broken, even if only to a minor degree. The participants can then connect and empathise with these characteristics of relating through the puppet plays, and stories which explore the complexities around trust and offer opportunities to rehearse different approaches and outcomes.

The basic structure of each workshop is the same and it is important that the workshop conventions are established right at the beginning and maintained. The sessions always start with an introduction, to be followed by a warm up and exercises and games which prepare for the interactive work of improvisation and dialogue, and the stories and plays which are the substance of the work. Each workshop closes with a debrief which is essential and must never be missed.

The introduction to each session states clearly what that workshop is about, with a review of the past workshops, and explains where the current workshop fits into the overall design or 'map' of the workshop journey. Giving the participants clear, practical information right from the start provides a solid foundation for the success of the workshops and gives them the secure means by which to feel more powerful.

Next come warm up exercises and simple games with which you may already be familiar. The point here is context and how and why these games and exercises are being played, and for what overall objective, as each game or exercise anticipates and resonates the central theme of session. All the games and exercises have names, many light-hearted, so that both the facilitators and participants can identify them easily and refer to them. For instance, a physical exercise which appears in several warm ups, involving a tumbling down through the spine and a recovery through the spine to a poised standing position, is called *The Relax Button*, a name especially invented especially for younger participants. A memorable name can be useful – many familiar games, like *Grandmother's Footsteps*, have lively and interesting names – and, of course, all names given here can be replaced by others according to what you, and your group, would prefer.

Listening is a skill the workshops hope to nurture, along with the ability to value difference. The stories and plays, always told by puppets animated by the facilitators, are a means towards both. They tend to come in the second half of the workshop or towards each session's end, when the group has worked hard on exercises, games and discussions and may be tired. Sometimes they are the catalysts for discussion and brainstorming; sometimes they present a dilemma which the group considers and tries to resolve; at other times, they exist purely as short pieces of narrative or theatre, intended to bring the group together in a collective experience which reflects the themes and content of each workshop.

As the content of each workshop is powerful, each workshop demands and needs the safe practice of a proper closing section, so that each participant can leave the working space, alive with the issues of the workshop but debriefed, poised and ready to concentrate on what the next part of their day has to offer.

Language and multilingualism

As trusting and becoming authentically powerful are intrinsically linked to language, one of the most fundamental concepts underlying these workshops and the plays is their relationship to language and to languages. They are both structured to be used multilingually, although, of course, multilingualism is a choice.

Learning language and then learning to use it is, in great part, a child's means to power. Written and spoken language can be confusing and precarious media, even in your own first language. Not so play. It is spontaneous. And not so the non-verbal languages of the senses and the gestural languages of action, and the emotions which are the biological and psychological languages of our shared humanity. If the ability to play has already been impaired or lost in some participants, however this has happened, the workshops and the plays – for that is what these short passages of organised dialogue are, play – will help to restore it and confidence.

To be deprived of language, as anyone who has worked with refugee communities, with those who have lost speech, or who has themselves direct experience of not knowing the dominant language will know, is to suffer a loss of perceived and expressible identity.

As language also carries the cultural and societal frame of reference as well as having semantic significance, not to be understood or to understand precipitates that person, child or adult, into a strange world of markers, guesses, and dubious equivalents. It is very hard to learn when lost. Awareness around language is access to education. The most important imperative in this area is the desire to communicate and to respect difference so that concepts from different cultures are laid side by side, with neither better nor worse than another. If possible, the facilitators of these workshops would be familiar with the different cultures represented in the workshops, including those not only of race and language but also those of different ages. Some concepts do not translate into other languages because of cultural differences and it is extremely helpful to be informed about this.

Multilingualism and the relationship of spoken language and body language can not be written down easily. While not all gestures are universal – for instance, in Greece to wave with an open hand is an insult and in Japan 'me' is indicated on the tip of the nose – most are because they express emotions and emotions, although not what causes them, are the same for all humanity. If there is a failure of relationship or understanding, change the means of communicating: draw, mime, show pictures, make sounds – anything to relate – which method, in deaf culture, is called *Total Communication* and has much to teach the hearing world. Finding any means to communicate is completely relevant to the issues of the workshop and the plays, some of which consider secrets and being silenced, an almost inevitable feature of abusive situations. Overcoming the fear of not being correct linguistically is, in this context, a great leap towards safety. Indeed, those for whom speaking out is not easy are tragically very often those most vulnerable to forms of abuse.

Whatever language or languages are used to facilitate the workshops, care needs to be taken of the actual choice of key words. Someone taking part in the these workshops is called a 'participant', a word one hopes neutral enough to describe anyone, young, adult, elderly or with special needs, not just Fourth Year primary school students aged between eight and ten, for whom these workshops and plays were originally designed. Similarly, 'responsible' connects the participants with the consequences and implications of power rather than a less complex choice of word, such as 'careful' which could, because of its apparent simplicity, lead to subtle misunderstandings. Another reason to be thoughtful about language is that in abusive situations, its meaning can be distorted or changed as a way to take another's power. Placing words accurately, even though they might be sophisticated, and matching those words with a real desire to communicate will make the workshops accessible and provoke the curiosity and interest of participants.

Language which gives words to participants empathetically, empowering them to express themselves more, thereby becoming more themselves, is the opposite to what can be termed pedagogic language. Pedagogic language enforces attention, as in 'be quiet,' 'shush', 'listen', and polarises things that have no inherent morality into good and bad, nice and nasty, such as 'a nice, big stretch' and 'a nasty, dirty floor'. Other examples are 'should', 'ought', 'right', 'wrong' which all contain the implicit value judgement of the adult speaking. The example of a communication-enriched environment helps the participants focus much more than commands for attention.

Words are very powerful, some more than others, especially when working with younger participants; for example, 'bum' will nearly always cause a ripple of giggles and for a few of the participants, the mere mention of a trigger word such as 'power' will be enough to set them off flexing their muscles or mock-fighting their neighbour. By simply being aware of this possibility, this automatic response can be sorted out, leaving the participants more relaxed and open to the content of the workshops and plays.

It is suggested that the first words of the workshop are in a language other than English in order to establish from the outset that difference is welcome. The use of non-language-based games with other languages stretches the concept of what listening means. Without understanding Bengali, for instance, a participant can, by listening in the fullest possible way to the tone, movements and gestures of the facilitators, follow them as they set up a game in that language. Without listening in its usual sense, but through using eyes, face, hands and body, a participant can begin to understand and then learn to use other languages. When setting up exercise in one language, it is nearly always possible for a participant who does not speak that language to join in fully, since the majority of the exercises and games do not depend on spoken language. The exercises and games are easily adapted into other languages, especially those that have a key phrase as part of their mechanics, such as *Yes, Let's!* in *Communicating*.

However, most of the plays and stories need bilingual presentation or translation to make them fully accessible. If any of the facilitators are able, they may present the material first in a language other than that which is dominant, and then in English. What this does is to reverse the power dynamic for a change, and enormously enhances the self-esteem of the participants for whom English is a second language. Another way of making the stories and workshop discussions accessible is to involve the help of multilingual participants. In one school in which these workshops took place, a Somali boy communicated in Arabic with an Arabic-speaking peer who, speaking more French than English, preferred to talk in French with a friend who was bilingual in French and English. This friend then translated this into English for me and the rest of the group. What is being done is modelling – and therefore validating – the multilingual co-operation which some of the participants in multilingual groups will practise anyway, although probably informally in most other circumstances in which the group might find themselves. It is not helpful to depend invariably on the participants for translation. This means an important impetus in communication is being avoided or denied, and the common ground which is so moving when a group creates it for themselves is not being shared but simply used.

The puppets

When a person is disallowed their rightful, authentic power or their power is usurped, that loss represents a critical move towards their being rendered an 'object' by their abuser. To occupy the centre of your life fully is to experience yourself as being subject in your own life. These two ends of the continuum of identity are central to the use of the puppets, both in the workshops and in the plays.

The distinction between story and fact is another important contour of the map of protection and the journey towards full selfhood and the realisation of one's own power. It is very hard to function in a meaningful way when that boundary is blurred, as it is when truth has become a casualty in a complex situation which will often have the urge towards powers as its imperative. In the devising and design of this Trust and Power work, the puppets represent an totally unambiguous visual and active signal that story is being used as distinct from the interactive games and exercises. It is of utmost importance that this clarity is upheld, even when, exceptionally, the puppets are used as catalysts for some of the exercises, or more specifically as part of brainstorm discussions.

Puppets, like masks, have a curious ability to seem to express emotions, thoughts and personality. The colour puppets used in the workshops are easily-made glove puppets, androgynous, with bald heads of papier mâché, bodies of strong canvas, painted with bright geometric designs in acrylic paint with their name colour predominant. Small mitten-like hands, also painted in their own colour, can be sewn or inserted in the arm sleeve. In shape they are identical to the template given for the paper puppet bodies, only larger. The dragon can be made according to any design as long as it is not very fearsome-looking and can be painted any colour desired, whilst the elephant is identical but has tusks made of wire, covered with papier mâché and a silver cloth body.

Unless it is unavoidable – for instance, you are facilitating the workshops alone with a group that is too big to allow otherwise – never let the participants hold the puppets, although this is something all or most of the participants will long to do. The puppets are greatly sought after by most participants because, being objects that are animated, they acquire a certain kind of magic. Holding the puppets robs them of their magic, and everyone will grab at the participant with the puppet unless this is very carefully set up as part of a story or exercise. The puppets need a safe place to be taken from and returned to unscathed. A bag for the puppets or some other container, like a chest or box, also adds an element of surprise. Having a bag to put them in, however simple, makes it very clear when they and their magic are working and when they and it are not. The bag becomes another boundary. It becomes a neutralising place, a kind of home.

As will be seen from the directions in the stories and plays, the facilitators use the puppets and hold them in different ways. The first has been called, for the purposes of these workshops, the advocacy mode. In this way of working with the puppets, the facilitator holds the puppet on their chest, a little like a baby, with the puppet whispering into their ear. When a facilitator speaks for a puppet and acts as an intermediary between itself and the children and other puppets, it is called the advocacy mode. In this way of relating, the puppet will only communicate directly with the puppeteer. Next, the puppets are presented as characters from a story that the facilitator wants to narrate, so they become, like any actor, any number of people, children, grandfathers, friends and teachers. Their next progression is when they start to speak for themselves. They become Red, Yellow, Blue and Green, held by the facilitator in general sight of the audience of participants. Their final stage of relating is when they appear as themselves, with the facilitators now animating them out of sight.

As will be seen, some of the stories have a painful or upsetting quality. Were the facilitators to act out their stories without the agency of the puppets, the audience of participants would be liable to feel they had to take emotional responsibility for these adults. Putting a participant, especially a young participant, in this position would create anxiety. The virtue of the puppets is that they can enact incidents and comment on them but when they are taken off the hands, they revert to object status and any anxiety which is aroused is immediately grounded; the focus can stay on empowering and enriching the participants and their self-esteem.

If possible have a different puppet for each character in a story or play, but if this cannot happen, it won't affect the overall effect of the story. Act out or adapt the puppet plays and stories according to how many facilitators there are.

The puppets therefore make their own journey, which is emblematic of the journey of the group. This fact exists as a feature of the workshop design, and works at an intuitive level. It does not matter that the participants may not apprehend this consciously. In the first use of story, *Jam Sandwiches* in *Trust*, they relate their dialogue and stories through the advocacy of the facilitators who become narrators. Their next move is to be actors telling and performing the true stories the facilitators, still narrators, want to tell. These stories and plays, even if they are about the facilitators, are told in the third person. In other words, the facilitators never become the puppets. This would be regressive. Gradually, as the worships proceed, the puppets forge a direct relationship with the participants themselves, and start to tell and act out their own stories – reflecting the move from 'object' to 'subject'. The puppets the participants next make parallel, in a reflective way, the movement of the original puppets. For a small amount of time, these paper puppets confer on participants a carer status, allowing the process of taking care of ourselves and others to happen which, in miniature, is easy then to observe at this small distance and its qualities to integrate.

The template for the bodies of paper puppets which the participants decorate and make into their own is provided in *Body*. Their making could be incorporated into a session between the workshops of *Power* and *Body* but it is more exciting if their paper bodies are prepared beforehand and they are made as part of the session. These simple paper puppets are made out of sturdy coloured paper and animated by the insertion of a ruler or small hand after being decorated and named by each participant. The participants then have their own vehicle to say through the puppets what they may not or cannot say directly. The puppets, being easily invested with power and just as easily returned to object status again, can express with safety and control anything the participants want, including some of their most intense feelings, fantasies, and fun.

The stories and plays

Stories and plays present the world as ordered, even if their content and style are fragmented, which in these pieces, they are not; they are the world-as-idea, the world of 'what if this happened to me', presenting even painful and true material in a way in which experience has honed the past and made it tellable, although perhaps still unresolved. There is saftey in story for it provides a 'third island' in which the narrator and theaudience meet, where shared dilemmas, conflicts and outcomes can be explored together through the medium of the characters and the commentaries. In the stories and plays, then, issues and experience which may as yet be beyond the participants' power to articulate are offered up for scrutiny, re-telling, discussion and often, for revision and the rehearsing and acting out of a variety of solutions.

All the stories and plays written and developed for the Trust and Power workshops are presented here, including alternative choices in the section *More True Stories* and in *More Plays For The Colours*, each one of which can be used separately but which together form a narrative sequence. These plays were written after the first Trust And Power workshops and incorporate many of the actual responses of the participants. Although all the material has gone through the writing and structuring process which in itself is a kind of transformation, great care has been taken not to distort or soften them. They have been performed, both professionally and in workshops, before many audiences both in the United Kingdom and internationally and have received praise for their authenticity and ability to touch their audiences.

With the exception of the first story, *Jam Sandwiches*, whose function is to introduce the fantastical elephant and dragon puppets to each other and the participants, all the stories and plays are based on real experiences or are a fusion of more than one true story. Some stories, such as *Nadia's Grandfather*, are told from the perspective of time, and encapsulate their own resolution. Others, like *Mina's Kitten*, will engage because they relate injustices that stand in time but which can provide grounds for sympathy, thought and learning.

The rationale for developing narrative material out of stories rooted in truth was to provide a genuine touchstone of experience. The fact that these stories actually happened earns the participants' respect. If you do decide to consider using your own experience as a catalyst, making up stories and plays of your own, the personal nature of the origin of stories and plays and the reasons they have been chosen will be very clear to you and therefore the participants. All the stories can, of course, be changed and adapted as necessary or replaced with stories that are more appropriate to the participants' situations and culture. However, whether they are altered, left the same or replaced by new stories, they do need to illustrate clearly the learning goals of the original curriculum on which the workshops are based (which can be found towards the end of this book). Be careful when you devise your own stories to be honest, appropriate and not to fudge or soften the past in order to make it better. You may find working directly onto a tape recorder helps the story or play have freshness and simplicity. You must also be sure that you understand the past and are ready to contribute your experience in this way so that you do not pass on unresolved anxieties, anger or grief. This would be to place an undue burden on the participants. 'Telling your story' is a fundamental theme of the workshops and plays, epitomised by the use of true stories, but it must be stressed that this is not always an easy thing to do.

The difference between a story and a play in the workshops is that the stories have a intensively subjective point of view, while the plays tend to be more balanced in terms of the protagonists, with the action of the story shared more equally between them. Although some of the plays and stories are written for two narrators, referred to as Narrator One and Two, in most cases the plays and stories can be told by one storyteller. Neither the stories nor the plays need to be learnt. If you decide to use the stories given here in the workshops, you can tell them in your own words, if you like, or read them from a script on your lap. It will make only a small difference to the audience because they will be focusing on the puppets rather than on their manipulators.

Preparations for the workshops

Undertaking these workshops will represent a significant commitment to safety and self-esteem in any organisation within which they are implemented. As with the workshop facilitation, the foundation of their success lies in giving clear, appropriate information to all parties concerned, and doing that well in advance of the workshops taking place.

These six drama workshops, which have a transforming ability, may be planned and executed in liaison with professional agencies: for example, in conjunction with training initiatives around anti-bullying; any developmental work on improving the ethos of the initiating institution; and on empowering individuals and organisations to overcome anxious resistance and to use those residual fears creatively to set up responsible processes for working with groups around safety and protection issues.

Curriculum planning is important. These workshops need to take place in an information-rich context. The participants will already have been given age-appropriate facts about safety and similarly pertinent sex education in curriculum work on person and social education.

Each institution or organisation will have its own unique way of preparing for these workshops but all should write to the parents and carers of younger participants to let them know about this initiative. This is for the safety of all parties concerned. The workshops can only take place effectively in an environment in which its staff and concerned adults have training in child protection issues, and it should be clear to all staff whom to make contact with if and when they are worried about a participant, and what the arrangements are if any participants should disclose information about abuse of any kind and specifically about sexual abuse. It should all be clear from the outset of this programme that while confidentiality will be valued it cannot be guaranteed, especially if information comes to light which is disturbing enough to be passed on to other professional agencies.

The participants need to feel that they will be given as fully informative an answer as possible to any difficult or awkward questions they may ask . Should there be a disclosure, no organisation should have to deal with those challenges without having had training and without clear procedures for referrals in place. Immediately after a crisis or trauma is not the time to find out how to manage it, as so often happens in crises of bereavement and after incidences of eruptive violence.

Initial preparations will be determined by whether these workshops are to be facilitated by an outside agency, such as a team of drama workers or similar specialists. In that case, the situation will be of a group of adults coming into a milieu already enmeshed with its own dynamics and relationships. The agency must be comprehensively briefed about the workings of the organisation or institution, and the whole organisation must be made aware of the facilitating group and their background in parallel with the workshops and their content. If a team from within the organisation is to facilitate the workshops, then all other staff, including ancillary workers and management should be informed of this and, similarly, of the project details.

The benefits of an outside agency coming in to to do this work, given that they are skilled and experienced, is that those individuals who usually work with or teach the group which is to embark on the workshop journey have the opportunity during the sessions and their preparation to talk about the participants. They can share their responses about the group with the facilitating team and can also observe the participants freshly during the process, thus alleviating problems that come from entrenched relating, and the blunting of positive expectations. This is one of the most moving, and in some cases, mutually astonishing features of these workshops. Sometimes both the participant and those caring or educating them need a refreshing surprise. This can happen, of course, when the workshops are facilitated from within the organisation or institution, but then it will probably be the unfamiliar process and the content of the workshops which will excite that energetic freshness which always accompanies a real growth in self-esteem.

If an outside team are brought in for this work, they should meet the group or groups they will be working with before the workshops start and introduce themselves, and begin to establish a relationship. It is helpful if this is not a formal meeting but takes place where the participants are working or in a space with which they are familiar.

Systems of communication should also be in place if an outside team is facilitating the workshops for their access and use. They will then know how and to whom to pass on any responses, incidents or information that gives grounds for concern and to do so in writing. In exceptional circumstances, work on trust and power can trigger or reveal negative and potentially harmful interaction between the participants and their teachers or carers. In this unlikely event it is suggested that the team should again document what they have seen in writing and give it to the person designated to take responsibility for this sort of situation. While extremely disturbing and upsetting, like all incidents of abuse, it is better than that it come out into view than it should continue to exist in a covert and therefore potentially more damaging way.

This work with identity and its links to the two most significant elements in the workshops of trust and power will sometimes call up a degree of anxiety, if only residual, in its facilitators and those connected with the workshops. It is essential that all facilitators should have some form of supervision and be able to talk to another skilled person about any issues these workshops raise for them both personally and professionally. It must always be remembered too that it is better to make mistakes in the effort to support a participant, than for that participant to endure the suffering which results from the deleterious effects of their predicament being ignored and their needs unmet.

In disseminating information about the workshops, the actual participants themselves should not be forgotten. Where possible, but without anticipating or spoiling too much of the surprise of this inactive drama journey, let them and any larger group to which they belong, such as the whole school community, know in advance about the workshops. This gives truanting members of the group a chance to consider attending and should encourage general interest. Any interest in the workshops should be tended and developed through the detailing of their arrangements and more about their elements; for example, the puppets, which may be talked about but only seen within the actual confines of the workshops and their process.

Finally, the time of the workshop sessions and their venue needs to be arranged, again with as much notice as possible to avoid any alterations, such as a change of place, which are unsettling. In working with a large group – for example a whole year in a primary school which may well include more than a hundred participants – a timetable will have to be structured which allows for groups of no more than thirty participants as an absolute maximum to do each workshop. This will mean that the workshops will be repeated and it is suggested that three workshops in any day is a maximum. Ideally, after what will surely be a significant period of planning, these workshops take place over a four-week period, the first week being for preparing, meetings and making arrangements, while in the subsequent weeks two of the workshops are facilitated, being repeated as often as necessary. This might result in a timetable as follows:

Week One   Meetings with the participants, facilitators and others directly involved with the workshop groups.

Week Two   Tuesday: The first workshop, *Trust*, repeated as necessary with each group of participants with a debriefing of the facilitators and those professionals who work with the groups;

Thursday: The second workshop, *Power*, repeated as necessary with each group of participants with a debriefing of the facilitators and those professionals who work with the groups;

Friday: Supervision for the facilitators.

Week Three   As above but with the *Body* and *Feelings* workshops.

Week Four   As above but with the *Communicating* and *Learning* workshops and with an extended debrief and evaluation for all those professionals concerned with the workshop groups on the final day of the workshop period.

The workshop materials and practicalities

The workshops involve very little financial outlay for the materials they use, but some parts of the workshop are labour-intensive, particularly cutting out the paper bodies of the participant's puppets as part of the preparation for the third workshop, *Body*.

Everyone involved in the workshops – facilitators, participants and any observers – needs their own name tag that they will wear for each session. Making the name tags, and decorating them for instance, could be a positive way of introducing the workshops and explaining a little about them. As will be seen from the description of the workshops and their content, naming and owning are of key importance and this significance, an intrinsic dynamic of self-esteem, goes on resonating at all sorts of levels. These name tags will help everyone respect each other because they give essential information about the owner.

According to the number of facilitators leading the workshops and how many participants, divide each working group, for instance, a class, into up to three smaller groups, decided well in advance of the workshops beginning. It may be that the participants in the smaller groups reflect membership of their smaller groups in their name tags, but this kind of detail will be best decided by the facilitating team and the staff of the organisation in which context these workshops are to happen.

As well as gathering together all the papers, pencils and brainstorming sheets and so on involved for each workshop, it is crucial that the facilitating team make a 'map' of the workshop sessions which will be used in all six at the beginning of each session. Again, each facilitating team will have their own design and approach for this simple resource. The only essential information it needs to bear are the names of each of the workshops in their order, linked to each other in some way, as a route would link cities. If possible, without loading the sheet with too much information, the names of each session should be written in at least two of the languages most commonly spoken amongst the group. If the workshops are to take place in a monolingual context, it is still valuable to have other languages reflected, as it helps the participants to determine their relationship to the world beyond their community in a positive, outward-looking way and affirms the value of difference.

By the time the start of the workshops approaches, the other teachers or staff involved in the organisation or institution will have been prepared for the workshops taking place. It will be helpful, and perhaps already part of everyday routine, to let them remind the rest of the staff of the organisation when and where the workshops are to start and to be clear about whether or not observers are to be allowed and, if so, how many can be admitted for each session.

The space that the workshops happen in should, if at all possible, be the same space for each of the six workshops, thus creating a familiar and safe environment that provides a backdrop of continuity to the variety of changes and developments that the workshops engender. The space should be large enough for the participants to be able to move within it quickly, freely yet safely, well lit, and with its own privacy. This last specification should never be modified. The participants must be confident when they are engaged on these challenging and sensitive issues that they cannot be overheard or overseen nor made vulnerable in any way because of the physical space in which they are working.

All the resources created in the workshop should be kept. Ideally, they can be put up on the walls of the room to show the progress of the 'journey'. If this is not possible, when resources such as the brainstorm sheets are collected, the group should be told what is going to happen to them and reassured that the sheets will be kept carefully and not thrown away. Even older participants express anxiety about the resources created in these sessions and want to know that they, the objects, like themselves, the subjects, are going to be in safekeeping. These resources form a valuable body of work that can be used in any follow-up work, or be part of a review of the project that is open to the others in the organisation who did not or have not yet been involved in the workshops, as well as being a permanent reminder of the actual workshop process itself.

Preparation of the facilitator

Taking care of ourselves, trust and power, protection and self-esteem all have as their shared focus the safety and development of the individual in relation to others. Before making significant and intense connections with others involved in the execution of these workshops and before beginning this complex and rewarding piece of work, take time for yourself. If you have read this far, read a little further, that is, read the whole of this section, then stop and think about yourself. Start by asking yourself the simplest of questions, like how you are feeling, what is foremost in your thoughts, how you are physically? For a few minutes, imagine yourself from outside, perceived by others. If you repeat your name, what does it mean to you? Get a sense of your own unique identity. Next, think of what you know you do well, activities you enjoy, what you are interested in, and hopeful of developing. Keep relaxed physically and let go mentally, and then gradually consider this project. Is it something you have initiated or have you been co-opted as part of a team? Why is it to be done within your group, organisation or institution? What are the expectations around it? It is especially important to try and sense these as they form a template for the project's outcome, a misty hidden agenda, and being aware of what hopes and potential disappointments are likely even before the work starts gives you, as a facilitator, protection, empowerment and clarity.

Next consider why the project is being undertaken. Whose permission was central to its going ahead? Who else is involved, and how do you feel about them? Do you know the participants yet? If not, when are you to meet them? Although you might be going to use this book simply as a resource to dip into and use as required, this scrutiny will be invaluable to you too, as one of the phenomena of working on self-esteem in this practical and inclusive way is that as it is approached, self-esteem, like a frightened animal, seems to vanish as soon as you start to look for it! With discomfort and amazement you can realise that you have no self-esteem at all or what does exist is extremely low until gradually it or you reasserts its presence. This is why it is essential preparation to confirm your sense of self before you begin to consider the issues of the workshops and their content, and how you are going to facilitate them.

Now let the questioning go to a different, more personal area. Because this work, which is for the benefit of the participants, can call up your own past, be careful to discern what rightfully belongs to you and what facilitating this work involves. Do you have a personal reason for undertaking work which involves building self-esteem as a means of empowerment and protecting against abusive experiences? Have you been abused yourself? One of our denial mechanisms is to reduce the severity of our past experiences so only others have really experienced abuse, what happened to us wasn't 'that bad' and we may feel slightly ashamed if we haven't 'got over it'. But if you know with utter clarity that you are a survivor of abuse, this will affect your facilitating of the workshops and make it different from the facilitator who knows with the same certainty that they have not been abused. If you have survived such challenges to your own self-esteem, you will have direct knowledge of the importance of such issues as identity, ownership and confidence in this area and they will need no explanation. Neither approach will be better or worse than the other, simply different, and each will bring with it its own expectations and doubts. The metaphor of a journey runs throughout this work. Knowing why you are doing it will always keep you from being lost, even if the work does become challenging and confusing. Hold on to your reason for undertaking it as surely as if it were a compass or touchstone.

Just as teaching is not about what is but what could be, expectations are crucial. As you start out, what expectations do you have? Of yourself? Of the organisation? Of the others in the team? And particularly, of the participants? Are any of these expectations actually possible to fulfil? One of the characteristics of those who have been hurt through abuse is the desire for perfection and being perfect. Because of circumstances beyond our control, some abuse has been perpetrated in the past and hurt us and our identity. The yearning for that not to have happened, for there to have been no spoiling, no breaching of boundaries, results in an extreme sensitivity to 'mistakes' as well as an inability to take any kind of feedback for every response, however well meaning, feels like criticism, and in the aiming for unobtainable standards. Having too high an expectation of yourself, the team and the group ensures the 'failure' of the project before the workshops even begin. Alternatively, especially if you already work with the groups involved, you may have a fixed expectation level for them, perhaps without being fully aware of it. This could be too low, and could prohibit new responses and the liberation of an authentic self-esteem which can help individuals to come closer to their own potential and to realise it. Less personally-based expectations, like those we all have, for example, around gender which are impacted with stereotypes, will also need to be surprised out of the way in yourself and in the group to allow for freshness and expansion, which is why, for the main part, the puppets themselves have no fixed gender and should be designed as androgynously as a teddy bear or a bird.

Following an appraisal or awareness of self-identity and expectation comes what is yours, what you own. Owning is a theme of fundamental importance to the workshop ethos because of its obvious links to power. Any kind of abuse in any degree can take away autonomy, innocence and power in some measure from its owner, leaving a great sense of loss which we often have to repress in order to survive at all. Therefore it is important to be clear about role-definitions and responsibility both for the process and for the content of the workshops.

The Trust And Power workshops, or indeed any work around taking care of ourselves in this way, can trigger off irrational responses around ownership in the other adults involved or touched by this project which they themselves, however learned or trained they may be, may not understand. It might be helpful here to be anecdotal. One of the family therapists involved in advising on the original prototype of the workshops asked to borrow one of the puppets for a conference presentation. The therapist chose Red, the puppet most connected to anger. Some days after the conference, I rang her office and left a message to ask for the puppet's return. I phoned several times without receiving an answer. Then the therapist did call back. Whilst knowing that puppets had been thought of and commissioned by myself and paid for out of my funding for the project, the therapist told me that Red was hers, they were kidnapping him [sic] and in fact all the materials of the workshop and the workshops themselves also belonged to her and her unit. I left the matter for another week or two, and then called again. As if nothing had gone before, the therapist made an appointment to return Red. She drove her car round to my office, and opened the boot to reveal Red who had clearly been there for some time. The puppet was only a little the worse for wear, with a couple of easily repairable scratches to its paint and was soon put back in the bag with the other puppets. The affair was 'forgotten' with the therapist being as friendly and supportive as ever. However, it was a lesson to me about the need for alertness, the depth of response provoked by the project, and the importance of ownership.

Sometimes when our self-esteem is low or delicate, which it can be when we are confronted by the new and the unknown, it is difficult to own and not to feel owned by a process. Owning the material is a form of empowerment. Once you decide to do the workshops, they and their contents become yours, to execute, change, cut, supplement, adapt or assimilate as you think fit. You own them, and therefore take responsibility for your part in them. Finding responsibility unbearable and unmanageable is, of course, another symptom of a self-esteem which is not strong or clear about boundaries.

As has been described above, all the stories in this book are true, and have been adapted very little for presentation in the workshops and for inclusion in these pages. The stories have been given by their owners to the workshops in full knowledge of their intended use and with their full consent. If you decide to develop some new stories, based on your experience or those around you, be very careful about ownership and give the full details of how these stories will be used before you start or you may find, once the stories are written down and ready to be passed on into the workshop process, that the owners of experience on which the stories are based can feel exploited, and that something that they own is being usurped and taken from them.

If you do undertake to devise your own stories and plays using your own or someone's else's real experience, identify the learning goal or point that you want to illustrate from the original curriculum the workshops are based on, which you will find towards the end of this book: for example, the need for privacy and not having to tell everyone everything. Next, consider that point without making any judgement on it. Let yourself think about that time when you had realised you could be private and that there was nothing wrong with that. Focus on the actual facts, not what could have happened or what you wish had happened, and then write your story straight down, or, if you prefer, dictate it into a tape recorder. If you are facilitating these workshops with others, an excellent way of working is for all of you to be present and for you to relate your story to another member of the group who can record it for you, or encourage you to write it down simply and quickly. The closer to how is was first written down, the most effective it will probably be. After having completed the writing, think how it will transfer into the third person to be enacted by the puppets and how you will use other languages, if at all. Alter and edit as necessary, but resist the temptation to tidy the incident or idealise it. It now forms part of the workshops to be shared by everyone. In some fundamental sense, it stops being your experience, becoming instead your experience used as a catalyst for learning and greater awareness. However, apart from these stories which form only a small percentage of the overall material used in the workshops, as a general rule do not share your own experiences with the participants, or you could risk making the participants responsible for you emotionally instead of the other way round.

If you do use a story from your own life, be sure that you really want to share it before you tell it and that the telling of it does not make you feel vulnerable or exposed. Introduce it as being yours, in the first person, but when the story proper starts and the puppet representing you is presented, go into the third person. This creates a useful distance which shows that you yourself have been able to reflect on it, and this allows the participants to do the same. If you use stories given to you by others, check if they would like you to use their names or if they would prefer the names to be changed. This does not represent a denial of ownership. The importance is in the experience and if someone prefers not to be named but wants to contribute, this is what makes them feel safe and is totally acceptable.

One of the primary objectives of the workshops is to listen nonjudgementally to the participants in order to build the most creative relationships possible. Sometimes that demand, together with everything else that may be going on in your life, will take you to the limits of your energy and capacity for neutrality because, inevitably, the issues that are being worked on will resonate in you, but you cannot give these feelings, thoughts or memories expression in the workshops as you are there for the participants and for others connected with the workshops. You need someone there for you. The need for some form of supervision, even if it is informal, must not be ignored as it is an essential part of this process of safety and care. Before the workshops begin, invite a sympathetic person not directly involved with the workshops but who has knowledge of the issues to listen to you and other members of the team as you plan this work. You can then set regular times for you and any other facilitators to meet with him or her on your own and as a group during the workshop process. In the Colours Play, Yellow has become an advocate for Red, Yellow and Blue, defined as someone who is on your side and who speaks for you if you want them to, which is why she does not tell her own story in these short plays. You need to know there is someone on your side in case you need him or her, even if you do not need anyone to speak for you. You will also want to talk about individual participants, both on your own or as part of the team. You may have very different perspectives on the same situation. Having someone in a supervisory role outside the running of the workshops will be to have objectivity and support.

As you approach the workshops and consider the material and what you will use, what change and what introduce, don't be tempted to censor or weaken the information that the existing workshop material carries. Don't select only the contents you think suitable and easily assimilated by the participants and ignore the more challenging aspects of the sessions and the stories and plays, all of which have been carefully designed to serve a curriculum. This workshop process is unusual. It may be that it and its information towards enpowerment can be understood most effectively in retrospect. Like buying children's clothes, they are large enough for the participants to grow into and they can and will be understood far beyond the timetable of the session. This is their protective nature, that they will last into the future and be there to be remembered when needed.

You will know from your own experience or from the training you will have had around protection issues that it is very hard for anyone who is or has been abused to break their silence and disclose their experience. They have often been put under pressure to keep whatever happened a secret and that secrecy is enforced by threats and fear. It is unlikely that any participant will disclose abuse to you, but in that event you may be asked to keep a secret. While confidentiality will be something you have thought about, you cannot keep secrets and you cannot promise that you will. You must be clear right at the beginning of any conversation that may lead to information being given to you that is about a matter that you will need help on and need to take further. It is to break the participant's trust to assure confidentiality and then not to keep it. Everyone who has been put under the pressure of secrecy because of abuse will know the intense relief of hearing these words: 'I believe you.' Nothing can be more welcome in that situation. If a participant discloses information which turns out to be false, they are nevertheless in distress themselves to be this needy of attention and so far away from the security of truth. You will also be aware from your training that in these situations, you should not ask leading questions, questions that can be answered with a 'yes' or 'no' and that all such conversations must be documented and shared with the appropriate person or authority as soon as possible.

Before starting the workshops, read all the material through. Although this might be demanding, it will help you structure the most appropriate sessions for your group, and will give you an essential overview of the whole process. Practically, the number of facilitators will determine much of the process. It is suggested that there is a facilitator for every ten participants, and that there are, at very maximum, thirty in one whole wokshop group. Obviously, if there is only you or if you are working with a very small team, many of the workshops activities will take longer, and this also apples if you are working with a large group. If you are on your own or working with a larger number in the group than you will wish for ideally, then select exercises and games which are easier to realise with one facilitator and do less.

The workshops often require the whole group to divide up into three smaller groups. Stay with that same group for the entire sequence of six workshops. This will develop continuity and a feeling of security that will not be disrupted if, for example, something unavoidable happens like the space in which the workshops take place is changed.

If you are new to the participants, learn names as quickly as possible, not only for those noisy participants but also for the 'invisible ones', who may want to wriggle from gaze.

Take risks yourself. Be expressive in your body language, even if this is embarrassing at first. You can only expect of the group what you are willing to do yourself. The same goes for using different languages. Overcome the fear of sounding ridiculous to yourself or of making mistakes. This is what the participants for whom English is a foreign language have to do almost all day every day. They will be sympathetic and supportive and this will create a helpful and creative working atmosphere. When the exercises or games suggest that everyone sits on the floor, sit on the floor youself, unless it is uncomfortable, thus supporting the notion that all of you are on the same journey, although, of course, you are in a different relationship to it.

Try to get across the reality that no one can fail in this work as it is not about right or wrong, good or bad, nor about failure or success. You don't even have to articulate this but simply act on it. Confidence and trust should begin to build up as a result of this firm but supportive approach. It applies to youtoo, although not as simply. So don't be frightened, say, of having the list of exercises you are going to use for each session as a crib. Put in any alterations or adaptations that you want to make, and have that piece of paper near you. No one will think the less of you.

Feel free to invent your own names for the exercises and games just as you may want to introduce new ones and ones that do not appear here in this book. When you choose someone to demonstrate an exercise, be careful that they will not be vulnerable and that you are asking them to do something that they are able to do. Don't alway choose the most confident or most willing participant. Choosing someone who exhibits low self-esteem to do an exercise with you can greatly lift their confidence and can contribute very positively to a more balanced group dynamic. Always thank someone who demonstrates with you. They are taking a risk and this should be acknowledged in thanks. Don't be afraid of repeating exercises. To repeat is often to develop. Give lots of positive affirmation during the exercises. Although this work is exciting and absorbing, some of it will be difficult and everyone, including yourself, should be encouraged where possible. You can encourage the participants, and you and the other members of your team can encourage each other but, more pertinently, can be encouraged by the person who is supervising you.

If an exercise does not work, take responsibility for this. It will be because you were not clear. The participants are not to blame. If, however, they are intent on scuppering an exercise, which is a different situation, try and put this response into a context. Why do they want to destroy concentration? What has made them, or certain members of the group, resistant? Don't ask them these questions. They are for your own due consideration. Give the exercise a good try, and then, using your judgement, go on to the next but do not omit to make it clear that the previous exercise did not work and that you may want to come back to it at a later stage.

Don't make anyone do anything they don't want to do. If someone does not want to join in, ask that participant why they don't want to do a particular activity, but don't press for a detailed answer if none is volunteered. The effects of the workshop go on above and below ground, as it were, and even if you can't see what is at work, it doesn't mean that nothing is happening. If you can accept objections without challenging them or agreeing to them, you often find that the participants will go ahead and do what they objected to anyway! It is as if they need to make their objections plain in order to be able to go ahead and act.

When planning the sessions, be careful of time. If you get involved in developing one exercise and run out of time for the rest of the exercises you have planned, it may not matter at all, but always finish the session with one of the debriefing exercises. This is because everyone, including yourself, needs to come out of role, out of the imaginative and emotional state of the workshop and return fully and sensibly to ordinary, everyday life so that you can all get on with what you have to do next.

Be sensitive to change, for instance, a shift, a re-balancing in the group dynamic. This is welcome change but it may be proceeded by a period of unruliness while the adjustment is taking place. Frequently, what seems like disruption or anarchy is just the harbinger of a turning point or breakthrough. At these times, you will need to be grounded, firm, and analytical, trying to understand what is happening, and what the change is from one state to another. Above all, always respect the participants, whatever their age or experience. If this respect is there whatever else follows cannot help but be beneficial and creative.

You may find that some participants leave you with very distinct feelings. One participant perhaps may always make you feel frustrated or enraged. Monitor your own responses. Often, in grief work, a young person will leave the facilitator feeling just as they feel – as frustrated, as lost, as angry. It is as if they are unable to express themselves by any other way other than making you feel what they are feeling. Again, these impressions are something you will want to share with the other members of the team and with the person supervising you.

All of us have likes and dislikes and will find some people more attractive than others. Monitor your own likes and dislikes in relation to the participants.

It may be you are drawn to a particular participant because they are, perhaps, very similar or very different to you, and that you tend not to like another because there is something in their lives which touches or resonates in yours. Be scrupulously fair and try to give everyone, whatever their needs, whatever you feel about them, equal time and attention.

Keep notes on the workshops and on any participants that may give you grounds for concern or joy. It is just as important to record and celebrate the positive events and contribution in the workshops as it is to monitor those that disturb. The workshops cause change and documenting them is another kind of useful map. If you repeat these Trust and Power workshops in the future, your notes will be invaluable and they will also tell you just what effect, if any, the whole process has had on you. Take care of yourself during the facilitating period. Give yourself approbation, flowers, some treat to mark your labour and if you are facilitating with others, do something communal which will support this care-taking.

Finally, it may be that you feel a particular participant needs special help or attention beyond the scope of your skills and the workshop process. Share this with the person who is supporting you. You may like to refer to the list of contacts in the back of this book and seek additional advice or help.

Facilitating the workshops

The workshops need to take place in a large space which is self enclosed – a hall is perfect. Before the start of the workshops, have all your materials ready, including, for instance, pins or other appropriate means of displaying the map of the workshops, the brainstorm sheets and the puppets. You will find a list of all the materials needed for any one workshop at the beginning of its chapter. Keep the hall light, warm, airy and clean, with the space in the centre as large and as clear as possible. Set up the Listening Corner in which ever corner of the hall is most convenient, but not facing the windows as this will make you and your team hard to be seen as the light will be behind you. Have the puppets ready in their bag together with scripts of their stories. Keep your crib of the workshop exercises easily in reach, and remember too that you and the team will need to be able to time the workshop accurately, so wear watches or have a clock in the hall.

The practical running of the workshop for most participants, especially those who are younger, will be prescribed by the institution in which the workshops are taking place. However, with other groups, it may be appropriate before you begin the workshop programme to negotiate some agreements which will govern all the sessions and their working. The kind of issues that can be discussed are punctuality, confidentiality, breaks, language, no smoking or eating in the shared space, parameters for feedback and responses, how to listen and to listen to each other, and how to relate to each other and the facilitators. The agreements, written down on large sheets of paper, are then clearly displayed in the workshops, but can be modified or added to at any at time, as the consensus demands.

The workshops take place in a zone of their own creating in which right and wrong are not the markers of behaviour that they are elsewhere. Within the sessions, and this applies to all participants, irrespective of age, there are very few rules. The first and most important is respect for each other, and that there is never the use of any kind of physical force in any circumstances. The second is that any adults entering the workshops to observe or for any other reason, has to introduce themselves. The content and the process of the workshop need to be identical, and it is not helpful in this delicate work around boundaries that 'strangers' should be free to enter and exit and watch without identifying themselves.

If you are working with older participants, don't be too anxious about the seemingly childish aspect of some of the exercises. Obviously, you will, by your tone and manner, treat these participants, whatever their special needs or specific backgrounds, with respect, but these exercises and games can bring out a child-like quality which is liberating. As the ability to play can be impaired by negative experience, the opportunities which these workshops give to older participants can also bring out the child within them, which is restorative and beneficial.

Don't be daunted if the exercises seem complicated. They sometimes take much longer to explain on paper than they do to do in a workshop and are actually surprisingly simple. Try to keep to an agreed timetable for each of the sessions. Getting behind time does cause anxiety and a concern about boundaries in everyone, particularly the participants. For instance, it might be useful on your crib to divide the contents into time zones so that you can see, if you do get behind, the extent of the delay so that you can always leave a proper period for the closing of each workshop which is essential, and if it means dropping something else, don't hesitate to do so.

Many of the games and exercises are predicated on simple and benign rules which must be kept. For instance, if you are seen to move during *Grandmother's Footsteps* you do have to go to the back of the room and start the approach to grandmother all over again. These games and exercises, with their simple non-coercive rules, are clearly set up and designed so that failure is not an anxiety because neither it nor winning enter into the workshop ethos. Because choice, along with information, is central to the issues of empowerment, if anyone doesn't want to participate in a particular piece of work, they need not do so as long as they give their reasons, but it would be good to know their reasons, if they felt like saying them; third, there is no right or wrong way to play the games or participate in the exercises and, of course, that is a powerful reiteration of the fact that no one's feelings are right or wrong either, a key point in the curriculum.

Documentation is important. However brief and sketchy, notes made at the time are eloquent in their immediacy. Keep notes also on both the process of the workshops and on any participants that seem remarkable, perhaps because they reveal something of their internal struggles in a new way or because of dramatic increases in self-esteem or communication skills.

All the resources created in the workshop should be carefully kept. Ideally, they can be put up on the walls of the room to show the progress of the journey. If this is not possible, when resources such as the brainstorm sheets are collected, the group should be told what is going to happen to them and reassured that the sheets will be kept carefully and not thrown away. Even older participants express anxiety about the resources created in these sessions and want to know that they, the objects, like themselves, the subjects, are going to be in safekeeping.

The book is a resource which can be viewed as a compendium of exercises, games, stories and plays. You can use them as you want, in part, in their entirety or singly, just using a story, or an exercise or a play as you wish. The choice is up to you. Although the workshops are given here in full, that is to give you a wider choice and to allow you to find something which really is appropriate to your own specific situation and aims. Adapt what you have chosen to your own needs but always begin with a warm up or introduction and close with debriefing exercises.

As well as documenting the workshops themselves, look after the resources created in the workshops, especially the puppets. They could be of great value to your community in ways which may not be clear at the time. The exercises and games can, of course, go on being played long after the workshop sequence has been completed, and the stories and plays can go on being told and presented. Sometimes it is very easy to see change in the participants and an enhancement of self-esteem, but sometimes it is hard to be optimistic. The truth is we just don't know what will be of importance to these participants in the future and whether any of the work we have done will be of any use. But we did it. That's the main thing. And we were there.

CHAPTER 3

Workshop One: Trust

The success of a journey depends on its beginning. Only if we have trust can we go on a journey, and we can only go as far as our trust will let us for when we feel unsafe, we stop. Trust is security. In this first workshop, a safe space is created in which the participants can work. This is achieved through giving them clear, accessible information about you, the workshops, and what the participants will be doing and why. You are inviting the group into a relationship of trust, a capacity we all have the potential for, but it have may already have been damaged in some of the group. Trust is to believe confidently in something or someone; it is also to act when an outcome is unknown. Both these definitions are made and applied throughout the session. As with any work, the higher your expectations are of the participants being able to explore and travel, the greater the likelihood that they will

Using imagination to create the future, minding about things, learning to make mistakes and take risks can result in a general raising of self-esteem, both of the group and its individual participants. All are to be found in this workshop which, being the first, establishes its conventions and those that follow. There will always be an introduction, a warm up and, whatever happens in the middle of a session, a closing. As this is a very full workshop, it may be that you will not plan to do every exercise or tell every story, but use at least one or two of the exercises in each part.

The initial four exercises prepare the group for what lies ahead by warming up the participants physically and psychologically. The next three exercises develop the participants' skills of responding and listening, not just through hearing but also through sight and touch. Through these simple games, the group dynamic can be shifted and harmonised and concentration enhanced. Trust games follow which require the participants to take responsibility for another. In pairs, the group literally learn to lean on each other and to guide each other. The focus then shifts from the participants as subjects of the workshop, in that they are working subjectively, to objects that the participants create in mime and remember through mime. Emotional memory is also stimulated as the capacity to care is acknowledged. In the final part of the workshop, fear, implicit in the concept of trust, is explored in tandem with how trust is built or can be broken. In the Listening Corner, the participants meet the puppets for the first time, watch them act out a short puppet play about building trust through overcoming the fear of difference and hear stories about trust being broken, which, dividing into their small predetermined groups, they then reflect on and discuss. Coming back together again for the closing minutes offers an opportunity for questions and comments before the participants receive positive affirmation of their work from you which they surely will have deserved.

Workshop One – Trust

Contents

- the 'map' of the workshop sessions
- the elephant and dragon puppets and the colour puppets

Introduction to the first workshop   5 minutes

Sit down and, if possible, without words, indicate to the participants to sit in a circle. Once the group are seated, greet them in any language other than their own, or in as many languages as are frequently spoken in the group, then in English. If you are not known to the group, introduce yourself and say something about you and where you come from and what you do. Any other adults present now introduce themselves. Go round the circle quickly finding out each participant's name, even though they will also be wearing their name badges. Hold up the 'map' with the names of the workshops on it. Explain this is the first of six drama workshops, each one-and-a-quarter hours long, each different. It will be like going on a journey together and this is the map. The workshops are about trust and power and how to keep safe and feel confident. Read out the workshop names, preferably in more than one language, and tell the participants this first workshop is about trust. If the group are not already known to you, go round the circle and find out everyone's names. Ask them if they are ready to start. If they are, stand, as they are going to do some acting and need to do exercises to prepare for it.

Warm up   10 minutes

1.1   Shake and Freeze

Using little or no verbal commands, lift your arms and shake them. Stop, freeze. Then shake them in a different direction, manner or rhythm. Stop, freeze. The group will follow you. Extend movement into the legs, the trunk. Stop, freeze. Be playful. Repeat once more. Come to a definite stillness. This opening exercise is very short and concentrated, not in itself having much need to be reflected upon, but sowing the seeds of later conscious consideration of what bodies like doing, what makes bodies feel good. Another function is to give the group an experience of working spontaneously and collectively, particularly in terms of timing.

1.2   Warm Up Faces

Now the bodies are warm, faces are next. Gently massage your face, asking the participants to do likewise. Screw up your face and relax it. Shake your head, letting go of any facial tension. Chew imaginary chewing gum and gradually stroke the face into being open and calm. One of the effects of abuse or any kind of enforced secret-keeping is a distortion of body language. This exercise can soften habitual tensions letting the participants' faces be expressive.

1.3   Relax Button

This simple relaxation exercise combines release with security. Stand feet apart, feeling the ground, with the knees slightly bent. Ask everyone to imagine they have a relax button at the base of their spine, and show where this is. Keeping the legs firm, press your own relax button, and relax the top half of the body into a hanging position, with the neck free and the head heavy. From this drop, slowly unwind the top half of the body, one vertebrae at a time, back to the vertical – the head coming up last of all. The exercise is strengthened by doing it in unison so ask the participants to locate their relax buttons, to press them, to relax over and then slowly to unwind. Repeat this two or three times. Watch the group, both to check that everyone has understood it and the spines and necks are free of tension. Notice if there are any very stiff necks and heads. Here, the participants are not trusting themselves enough to to let go. This might be because they want to keep an eye on the others or on you; it might be through wariness, fear of being caught off guard, or fear of looking foolish. Look out for the 'complete flop': when a participant, for some reason, perhaps misunderstanding the movement, or wanting to show off, or not feeling secure in themselves, collapses their whole body on to the floor. Some participants may have trouble literally 'standing on their own two feet' but as the workshops progress it will be possible to see improvements in balance and physical calmness. Difficulty with an exercise such as this may indicate a lack of ease in the participant in their relationship with peers, with adults, with their own body or the own sense of self-esteem. In any case, the exercise will be repeated in later sessions with more opportunities for freeing up and releasing.

1.4   Breathing 1

This brief breathing exercise blows away the tension, relaxes the face and mouth and centres the breathing. The exercise is done to a rhythm: time the in-breath by signalling one, two, three, a visual communication, underlining the point that the teacher or facilitator's voice is not the only organising principle. Demonstrate, breathing in through the nose, making the count very clear. This counting of the duration of the in-breath also helps to make it deeper, avoiding tension in the chest. First, breathe in for three and then release the breath in a big sigh. Repeat at least three times, encouraging the sighs to be bigger and deeper with each repetition. Watch that air is really being drawn down into the lungs and is not held with the shoulders pulled up and rigid. Participants with troubles and stress are often tight in their upper chest and cannot let the diaphragm work as it is too near the site of the solar plexus, the seat of the emotions in the body. This simple exercise will be developed throughout the six workshops.

Listening   **10 minutes**

1. 5   Clapping Round the Circle

This is the first of three circle exercises with the aim of working on specific learning points related to the theme of trust. Trust begins with listening, not only to words, but to touch, sensations, feelings, ideas and intuition, and, as is shown here, by 'listening' with the body and eyes. Have the group sit on the floor once more and join them. Hold your hands in front of you. Explain that you are going to send a clap round the circle, and be clear which way round the circle, clockwise or anticlockwise, you are going to send it. As soon as you have clapped, the next person in the circle claps, and then their neighbour and so on. The intention is for the clapping to sound like one person clapping quickly. It helps to look at the person next to you all the time and have your hands ready. Listening with your eyes, as soon as you see them clap, you can then clap. Be careful that the rhythm doesn't get uneven, with participants clapping prematurely or at the same time as their neighbour. Ask how the participants listened to know when to clap? Answers can include observations like they listened with their ears, or just 'felt' it. Choose someone to start another round, going the opposite way. If this has gone well, now try it with eyes closed. This makes the exercise harder and, for some participants, simply closing their eyes demands trust enough. Don't worry if the eyes closed variation cannot be sustained for a long time. The exercise's additional function is to begin to work collectively, intuitively and rhythmically. Again, this can all feel quite disorganised and risky but risk is one of the fundamentals of trust, for when we agree to act without knowing what the outcome will be, we do so on trust.

1.6   The Pulse

This exercise practises listening with the body as a means of communication, speed of reaction, and physical trust. Everyone stands in a circle and holds hands. Say that you are going to squeeze your neighbour's hand lightly. Then your neighbour is to squeeze his or her neighbour's and so the pulse will pass round the circle, just as the clapping did in the previous game. Some groups, especially younger participants, will really squeeze and even try to pulverise their neighbour's hand! Tell them not to hurt the hand they are squeezing, and also tell everyone to resist squeezing back the hand that squeezes yours. This inhibits the pulse from moving quickly and fluently round the circle. The aim of the game is to communicate freely and non-verbally. After the pulse has gone round a few times, and the technique has been established along with a degree of trust, stop and change its direction. Ask one of the group to start it off. Always get the person starting to be very clear about which direction the pulse is to go before sending it round. If the pulse gets lost, find out what happened to it and then try again. Notice how the pace quickens once the game is established. Ask how the participants listened to each other and find out if they are ready to try sending it round even quicker. If this goes well, do it with eyes closed, which, especially for younger participants, is not easy but this again invites the group to work together. This game introduces the idea that there are conditions attached to receiving and passing on a communication without distorting it, and that this involves trust. It also prepares for the next, more demanding game, and can give important information on participants who have difficulties in joining in. Ask what different ways of listening are used during the games? Suggestions can be: listening with ears, eyes, the touch of hands, listening to yourself, listening to your own feelings.

1.7   Movement Round the Circle

This is an extension of the Pulse, built up in the same way, following the same instructions. Instead of a squeeze, a simple gesture or placing of the hands is passed around the circle — for instance, a hand raised in the air or across the chest. Again for the first round all eyes are open, then closed in the second; hand-contact is maintained all the time. The idea is to pass on the movement as you received it, without changing it at all. If this works first time, and the gesture returns undistorted to its sender, elicit how everyone achieved it, for example, by being relaxed, trusting your neighbour, being attentive, accepting the gesture by 'listening' with your body. The distortion of information and communications is a feature of abusive situations. Being able to control, represent and pass on accurate information, even if it is only that of a simple gesture, is significant and creates confidence. The game may break down before a new gesture or a new direction of passing it, are tried. Breakdowns in the game could be because someone wilfully changes the gesture, is not clear, breaks the hand-hold or simply loses concentration and forgets to pass it on. It is not the results which are paramount, only the trying.

Trust exercises   15 m

1.8   Palm to Palm

This is the first of three trust exercises. Better than any words, they show the theme of this workshop. If you are facilitating with another adult or another adult is present who would like to, ask them to partner you. Otherwise, choose a participant closest in size and weight to you, or if this is not practical, one you can expect to be confident demonstrating something new to the group. Talk the participant through the following. Standing facing each other about a foot apart, place your hands vertically on your partners', palm to palm. Together, lean and accept some weight on your hands until you are in balance. Both of you should be feeling safe, with no fear of falling; neither of you should be sticking your bottoms out and thus withholding your leaning weight; finally both of you are ready to increase the distance between you. Move your feet back, but no further than feels safe. See how far you can go without toppling over or wobbling. Maintaining balance all the time, come back to your starting position, with each of you taking your own weight. Tell the group the aims of the exercise are keeping balance, trusting your partner, not letting your partner down, not pushing or tricking each other.

Now the group try. Pair up for this exercise so that the participants won't necessarily be working with someone they know – and trust or do not trust – already. This can be done by moving from the circle into two lines facing each other and then into pairs of opposites. This exercise is easier if partners are approximately the same height, although, with care, it can work with any couples. Ask how this exercise practises the giving and receiving of trust. The message of the exercise is that it is possible to build up a balancing trust with any other member of the group. Sometimes, pairs lose balance, overstretch, or break the trust. Overstretching can be seen as high spirits or lack of fear of falling, but notice the deliberate breaking of a balance, or more obviously, the reluctance to join in at all. Noticing all these different responses will give you significant information about such individuals and their possible diffidence in making and maintaining constructive relationships.

1.9   Wall to Wall

Continue with the same pairs as in the previous exercise to extend the relationship of trust. The action of the exercise is that one participant, with eyes open, guides the other, with eyes closed, from one wall across the room to touch the opposite wall. They then change places and go back to touch the original wall. The key to the exercise is in setting up and demonstrating it literally step by step. Be clear it is not a race but about feeling safe and achieving something together. Demonstrate. If you are facilitating with another adult, they let themselves be guided by a participant using his or her voice only – in any language – while they, the guided partner remain silent. If you are the only adult, finish all explanations before taking the role of guide. Do not attempt to be guided unless you are sure that the group is ready for this additional act of trust – that is of you closing your eyes! After the demonstration, ask the group what they think was helpful to the guided one and what made him or her feel safe. Some suggestions might be the reassuring voice of the guide, adequate warning of obstacles, precise instructions on the number of steps needed, not leaving silences and so on. Concentrate on positive comments so as not to set an example of criticism or complaint.

Next, two participants do the exercise, again with the group watching. This time the guiding partner can use touch as well as their voice. Reflecting on this development, note the additional need for a gentle but firm touch, guiding not pushing, a reassuring pace, and information. Finally all the pairs try it, all at once, putting into practice a learning process in which trust is built up gradually. Especially with younger participants, the exercise needs to be shown in stages. By the time someone has bumped their nose, it is too late for them to learn in a fully trusting way. If the learning comes through example first, it enables every pair to make a positive experience out of it. Also, the habit of competition is very entrenched, and need to be manoeuvred around carefully.

This game develops the theme of trust from *Palm to Palm* by making it less dependent on mutual self-interest (not falling). Although the equation – 'If you trust me, I'll trust you' – still remains, it is given a deeper and more extended context. On one level the game is between partners, between friends, and celebrates the possibility of building a trusting relationship. At another level, it acts out every human being's earliest history, the time when, as a baby, each of us trusted absolutely and indiscriminately. This physical memory can be quite a challenge for adults, for whom it can be a reminder of the amount of trust they have lost or had broken in their lives. Anyone who has experienced abuse may find it difficult to trust, to close their eyes and let someone guide them, since all their defences tell them never to trust anyone again. Learning to trust again, which is part of healing, can sometimes involve realising and then drawing on the resources you had before your trust was broken. For everyone, the experience of having someone trust you, and give themselves into your keeping even for as short a time as a minute, can enhance the sense of your own value. The exercise reminds you that once upon a time you trusted, with your eyes closed, and now, because of this, you can accept someone else's trust with your eyes open.

1.10 Precious Objects

In changing the focus from the participants themselves on to mimed objects, this next game is about trusting someone else with something which is precious to you. It also functions as an introduction to the puppets, the workshops' precious objects, and leads into an imagined reality where the puppets live, as subjects. Return to the circle, or two circles if the group is over twenty, and sit down. Start by eliciting the meaning of the word 'mime', for instance, acting without voice, creating imagined objects, not real ones. Notice this is the first time taking part in the workshop has been dependent on understanding a certain (English) word. If the participants have English as a second language, give a simple visual definition; for example, slip off a shoe and put it back on, then slip off a mimed shoe and put it on again to show what 'mime' is. You may want the group to repeat the word with you to add to their vocabulary and to tell you words for 'mime' in different languages which the whole group can learn.

Having established the definition of mime, mime an object, such as a necklace, and pass it to your neighbour who accepts it, its shape, size, function, and then changes it so that it becomes her or his own object – imagined in as much detail as possible. This participant, in turn, passes the new object, the ice cream, on to his or her neighbour, who, in turns changes it into a ball perhaps and so on. This exercise reprises the dynamic of the previous listening games but develops it into specifics, creating objects and subjects. The first round establishes the technique, and practises communication and clarity. Probably everyone will be very attentive, trying to identify what the objects are.

For the next round, the game is played as before, only this time tell the group the mimed object must be an object you once owned but now don't have – it might have been lost, stolen, or has worn out or been given away. It must be an object you mind not having now. Ask everyone to recall their object as clearly as possible. Allow a pause for this. Ask everyone to raise an index finger when they have thought of their object. Then play the game, only going round the circle once, with each participant miming and then passing on their own precious object. Almost invariably the quality of mime improves and the game is played more slowly.

After the round, ask the group what they felt. This is the first time introspection is introduced into the workshop. Point out you were being trusted with something precious (even something living in the case of a pet) by your neighbour and entrusted to accept the object, not to refuse, lose or destroy it. You in turn were trusting your neighbour with your own precious object. These two movements of trust are connected, and mutually reinforcing. To own there are things that matter to you that you no longer have is an act of trust because such an admission has a potential to make the 'loser' vulnerable.

Relating   30 minutes
1.11   A Time When

Still seated, ask the group to turn to their neighbour and work in pairs. For one minute each, one at a time without interrupting, first one participant then the other tell each other of a time when they were afraid or of a time when it would be useful to be afraid – in order to protect yourself. During this exercise, which is as much about listening as it is about talking, go round and listen yourself to the stories – in some cases, you may need to help the participants start off. When would it be useful to be afraid? If there is a blocking or refusing reaction, get around it by talking about someone else first, how they were afraid or their fear helped protect them. Blocking can often be a sign that there is something important going on which the participant is not ready to reveal yet, and this reticence should be respected. When the participants have finished, ask what, if anything, was different from normal conversation in this exercise? You might want to add that sometimes when people are scared, they are too scared to admit it. Now lead the group directly to the Listening Corner.

1.12   Puppet Play 1: Jam Sandwiches

Tell the group they are now sitting in the Listening Corner where they will be listening to the plays and the stories of the workshops and where they will be presenting their own when that time comes. Introduce *Jam Sandwiches*, a play about fear and the challenges of building trust. If you are facilitating the workshop alone, take both puppeteers' parts. Rani, the elephant puppet, will then only communicate through your left hand, body and ear while the dragon uses the right. Both puppets use the 'advocacy mode' (see the section about puppets in *About The Workshops*), communicating directly with their puppeteer in voices too quiet and shy for the audience to hear. In the play, the participants name the dragon. Naming and owning have special relevance to this workshop, which begins the journey, as well as to the whole sequence. This is illustrated again in this first encounter with the puppets. The puppets, precious objects, here become owned and animated by the group as subjects through the naming of the dragon, in this given instance, it is imagined that he is named Banzan. The participants are asked to contribute once more when they are asked how Banzan the dragon might overcome his fears and become friends with Rani. Listen to all the suggestions carefully and incorporate some of them into the resolution of the play. This is an example of commitment to enter into true dialogue with the group by trusting them for real and useful ideas which change and are reflected in the story. Both Rani and the dragon are shy at first, and unable to tell their own stories or address the group directly. This is to allow a movement of growing self-confidence in the puppets, as well as for the puppets to reflect the same kind of development from the participants. It is fitting that the group's first meeting with the puppets finds the puppets tentative, open about being afraid and reliant on the help of the puppeteers. This short play, running for about five minutes, will be understood by all participants, whatever their first language, especially if their body language is as expressive as possible. You can, of course, perform the play in your own words, but stick to its structure which has been carefully devised.

Jam Sandwiches

Puppeteers One and Two sit in front of the Listening Corner.

ONE: *(to the audience)* This is a play called 'Jam Sandwiches'!

TWO: *(to the audience)* As you know, often people are scared of things or of other people who are different, and because they are scared, they sometimes try to hurt them. Now you don't see many dragons about – probably for this exact reason. I came across this one – *(takes the dragon out of the bag and presents it)* – who was miserable and very alone. One of the last of the species. He needed a lot of looking after before he got stronger and got over being shy.

(The dragon grows less shy and looks directly at the audience.)

But he's great now...

(The dragon looks at his puppeteer.)

...and I could say a friend.

(The dragon speaks to his puppeteer.)

But he wants a name. He says people have only called him bad names, and now he wants one he likes. What do you think? What do you think he could be called?

(The participants suggest names for the dragon. He 'listens' to their suggests then chooses the name that he likes best of all, for example, Banzan.)

ONE: This is — *(Rani, the elephant puppet appears out of the bag.)* — Rani.

(Rani stretches and rubs her eyes. Banzan peeps at her, then hides as much as he can in the arms of his puppeteer.)

She's been asleep, haven't you, Rani?

(Rani nods. She looks shyly around her and speaks to her puppeteer.)

She's just had such a vivid dream.

(Rani nods excitedly and says more.)

Is that right? What happened?

(One tells the audience what Rani is telling her.)

You dreamed you were in a pure green forest when all of a sudden you saw a beautiful creature whose name you did not know, and who was unlike any creature you have ever seen before.

(Rani points fearfully to the dragon.)

What is it? Why have you gone all shaky? Yes, it's a baby dragon!

(Rani whispers excitedly in One's ear.)

O that's the creature you saw in your dream! That's extraordinary! What an amazing coincidence!

(Rani is friendly and wanting to go to Banzan. Banzan is terrified.)

ONE: Rani would like to meet…

(Banzan quakes.)

TWO: Banzan? Oh, but he is terrified. He's never seen an elephant before. Banzan, this is Rani.

(Banzan buries himself in Two.)

This isn't going to work.

(Two turns to the audience for help.)

What can we do? How can we help someone that is terrified?

(She listens to suggestions from the audience.)

ONE: We could sing to him. We could hug him. We could try and find out what she's scared of. Yes, those are all good ideas.

TWO: We could try and find out what he is scared of? Yes, that's would help, wouldn't it? He is scared of...

(Banzan buries his face in the safety of the puppeteer's shoulder, taking tiny little looks at Rani. Two turns to One.)

What's your name?

ONE: *(One says his or her own name.)*

TWO: Banzan, this is (...). Just have a look. If you can't face looking
at...

(She indicates Rani. Banzan shudders.)

...then listen. (...) is going to give you some information about Rani. See what you think...

ONE: Rani is an elephant. She has a trunk, and tusks. You can see them there, and she is very gentle and friendly.

(Banzan sneaks a look at her.)

I'll tell you some of the things we enjoy doing. We love going on long walks.

TWO: So do we!

ONE: Rani adores bananas.

TWO: So do we!

(Banzan is less shy and looking at Rani more directly.)

We go swimming. Do you like swimming?

ONE: Rani loves swimming, don't you? And she loves to eat.

(Banzan whispers urgently to Two.)

TWO: Oh that's what you are scared of... You think that Rani is going to eat you? No, don't be worried. She's vegetarian and anyway, do you think I would let you go near anything or anyone that I knew was going to hurt you? I wouldn't do that. You are precious to me.

(Rani speaks to One again.)

ONE: What does Banzan like to eat?

TWO:	Oh, almost anything.
ONE:	What about jam? Does he like jam?

(Rani squirms with delight.)

Rani does.

(Banzan squirms with delight.)

TWO:	Yes, Banzan does too.
ONE:	And you promise me he doesn't bite?
TWO:	You can trust me.

(Tentatively, Rani and Banzan greet each other.)

Banzan says 'pleased to meet you.'

(And goes on to greet her in other languages.)

ONE:	And so does Rani.

(Rani, through One, greets Banzan in different languages, as appropriate.)

TWO:	My feeling is – and I may be wrong – my feeling is, Banzan, that Rani could be a friend.
ONE:	By some curious chance, Rani and I happen to have some jam sandwiches in this bag…

(Banzan looks at her puppeteer and nods.)

TWO:	*(to the audience)* Banzan is not afraid now because we did find out what he was afraid of, and we did…

(Here the puppeteers incorporate some of the suggestions made earlier by the audience.)

…and it seems like Rani the elephant and Banzan the dragon are definitely on the way to being friends.

(They exit into the puppet bag, happy, hungry and together.)

1.13 Breaking of trust stories

Stories 1–3: Mrs Alvarez, A Packet of Opal Fruits, and The North Pole

Stay in the Listening Corner. Say that the play was about trust being made but now they are going to hear some stories, true stories, about the breaking of trust. In preparing for these workshops, you will, if facilitating, have already decided to tell a true story from your own experience, preferably about you directly, or to use one of the stories that follow. If there is more than one facilitator, listen to all the stories, three being a maximum. The puppets act out as much as possible of the story during its telling. The stories also show that the puppets can be used to act out any part or story. After each story has been told, each facilitator takes their own group, which has been prearranged, off into another part of the room. Ask the participants you are working with to tell you what happened in your story. In almost every case, they will be able to repeat it back to you almost word for word. Then go on to discuss the story with them, using the questions given at the end of each of the stories that follow as a guide. After this is completed, and be stringent about timing, come back to the Listening Corner where each facilitator gives a brief report on the discussions of their own group. If using *Mrs. Alvarez,* be sure to say in the report that it is against the law for a teacher to hit a student. You may also wish to use *Judy The Dog* in *Additional Stories And Plays* instead or as well as the stories below.

Mrs. Alvarez

NARRATOR: This is a true story that happened to Carol when she was eight. One day Carol…

(Presents blue puppet.)

…was in the classroom. Now it was summer, and it was a very hot day and the sun – you've got to imagine big, tall old fashioned windows, with the sun pouring through – was making Carol sleepy. It was near the end of the school day, Friday, last period. She was trying to do her work. It was writing and she wasn't very good at it. Then up came her teacher…

(Presents second puppet.)

…Mrs. Alvarez. Mrs. Alvarez looked at Carol who was sleepy. She said to her, 'Carol, you look sleepy. Do you want to go home?' Carol thought to herself, for she didn't understand that Mrs. Alvarez was not actually saying what she meant, Carol thought to herself 'that's the first sensible thing I've heard all week. I am tired. I would like to go home early.' So she turned to Mrs. Alvarez and said, 'Oh yes, Mrs. Alvarez. I would like to go home.' And Mrs. Alvarez didn't say anything, but…

(Mrs. Alvarez hits Carol hard.)

…but she hit Carol round the head.

- What happened in this story?
- How was Carol feeling?
- What did Carol think Mrs. Alvarez was suggesting?
- What did Mrs. Alvarez do?
- Now why do you think she did that?
- What do you think of what Mrs. Alvarez did?
- Did anyone do anything wrong in the story. If so, what?
- How did that make me feel?
- What could have made Carol feel better?

A Packet of Opal Fruits

NARRATOR: I'm going to tell you a story about a packet of Opal Fruits.
It's a true story about something that happened to Mina
when she was about eight years old. One day Mina…

(Presents green puppet.)

…and her two friends, Daisy and Rujis, …

(Presents puppets.)

…went to buy some sweets from the school tuckshop. Rujis
and Mina bought their sweets, but Daisy just took a pack of
Opal Fruits and slipped it into her pocket. Rujis and Mina
just looked at her –

(The puppets act this out.)

– they weren't too happy about what she'd done. Daisy
came up to them and made them promise that they wouldn't
tell anyone. They did promise. While they were eating their
sweets, Daisy ate up all of the Opal Fruits, and they did not
get any. But that afternoon Rujis and Mina had a long think
about what had happened and decided to tell Miss the next
morning. So they got to school extra early and told Miss
everything.

- What happened in this story?
- Whose trust was broken?
- Why did Mina and Rujis go to the teacher?
- Were they right to break their promise?
- How do you think Daisy felt?

- How do you think Rujis and Mina got on with Daisy after that?
- What could have made it better?

The North Pole

NARRATOR: This is a true story that happened to Kwesi when he was eight years old.

(Presents red puppet.)

Kwesi was eight and his teacher set everyone some homework to see who could come up with the best idea for a class project. Kwesi went home and thought hard. In the end, he came up with the idea of The North Pole. The next day, when Kwesi got to school, he met Paul Garner,...

(Presents puppet.)

...a boy in his class, in the playground. He asked Kwesi what his idea was. Kwesi told him he wasn't going to tell him. Paul told Kwesi his idea. But Kwesi can't even remember what it was now. Paul asked him again what his idea was. 'I'll keep it a secret,' said Paul. So Kwesi told him. Later that day in class, the teacher was asking everyone what their idea was. She got to Paul first. He said, 'The North Pole.' He'd stolen Kwesi's idea. Kwesi was really upset and didn't know what to say when the teacher got to him. He was sure the teacher thought he hadn't done the homework and he had thought about it so hard the night before. And 'The North Pole' was the project the teacher chose.

- What happened in this story?
- How did Kwesi feel?
- Who promised to keep a secret and why did they break it?
- Whose trust was broken in this story?
- Why did Paul suggest The North Pole?
- How could Kwesi have changed things?
- How could things have been better?

Closing   **5 minutes**

1.14   A Big Clap

Bring the group out of the Listening Corner back into the centre of the room, in a circle. Find out if any one wants to say anything, or ask a question. There will probably be silence which is fine. Ask them to remember back to *1.5 Clapping Round the Circle* and explain that they have done so well that you want to applaud them and ask them to applaud their own work before this first workshop about trust ends. Everyone claps. Remind the group when the next workshop is, and say that you are looking forward to it – to go on confidently expecting creative work from the group and to believe in them is to trust them and the process in which you are both engaged.

CHAPTER 4

Workshop Two: Power

After Trust comes Power. Implicit in trust is vulnerability and in power, strength. To make relationships is an act of trust. Power, a central issue in any work to do with protection and self-esteem, is what happens in relationships. To explore power, we need trust. Power is experienced in the effect we have on others and on our environment. Like trust, it has to be linked to responsibility for it to be exercised without usurping or impairing the well-being and safety of others.

Power has many connotations, some of them associated with positive inner capacities – of empowerment, confidence and endurance – but others stamped with images of physical strength, domination and violence. Power can be innate, made, reduced, lessened; it can be good, bad, harnessed, given, given up, taken or abused. Power is often equated with strength, particularly physical strength, but any kind of strength without responsibility can result in violence towards or oppression of others. This kind of behaviour is called bullying.

Anger is often mistaken for power, and while anger can fuel the desire to act in a powerful way, it is not the source of power. Power springs from the giving, taking and creating of information; and from different ways of understanding: intellectual, kinetic, intuitive and emotional.

This workshop is designed to reveal different aspects of powerfulness and carefulness: how power can change; how each person can be powerful in different situations; how powerfulness can grow or diminish; how rules and rôles can be more important than physical attributes in the whole arena of power. In it, feeling powerful is explored in all its senses, as is the crucial difference between feeling powerful and having power over someone. This is acted out in the games, exercises, story and discussion.

Each one of the participants will have their own unique sense of power, both in relationship to themselves and to others which, in part, reflects how the world and those in it have treated them. The dynamic of a group is the sum of its power relationships. All the participants are in a less powerful position than you and the facilitators therefore they, a group that already has some vulnerability, can only work well when there is some communality of power and when the group's individuals have some kind of feeling of power. At one end of the spectrum are the participants who have to overpower in order to get the attention they crave, while at the other are the 'invisible kids' who, although present, do their best to absent themselves and who find any attention unbearable. Different stimuli and different circumstances will make different participants feel differently. This workshop explores the issue of power and its safe application. It is a very energetic session and one that should result in a more harmonised group dynamic.

Before undertaking the workshop and in preparation for it, you may like to think of yourself in relation to power. For instance, among some of the questions you might consider are: Who has power over you? Who do you have power over? What is your power like in comparison with the participants? When did you last give power away? When did you last feel genuinely empowered yourself? When did you last rue a misuse of power? What could have been done to change that situation? What could be done now to ameliorate it? And so on.

Language is power, and the first eight can be played without an understanding of English, or whatever the dominant language is. Choice is power. Apart from the puppet play, all of the exercises or games have choice as the means of participating so that the participants can experience choice and power directly which is far more effective than complicated, verbal explanations. Language is powerful indeed, as you will see when playing Powerful Statues. Although some of the participants, particularly those of both genders involved in the macho zone, may look as though they could do with less power, not more, you may, through this workshop, be able to understand what influences lie behind these extreme defensive and emotional responses which are more triggered than deliberated. These participants react to the perceived threat of the word, in this case 'powerful'; and from your point of view this need not be negative. It opens up a space for a possible, though perhaps as yet, distant transformation, which wouldn't be the case if a more formal word like 'empowering' had been chosen. Being prepared for such eventualities means you will be able to contain them without their triggering other unwanted judgmental responses in you, like anger or disapproval.

The early exercises combine playfulness and power and question what true power is, as opposed to having power over someone. The brainstorms on power go on to focus on caring and being cared for, growing up, and by implication, they ask the participants to consider what activities and demands are appropriate to different ages.

The puppet play is about bullying. Being hurt almost always causes a loss of power, both to the injured party and to the person that inflicted the hurt. People without their own genuine and appropriate power and the choice it brings can be disruptive, defiant, stubborn, withdrawn or absent, precocious, hostile, violent and self-destructive because people who have been hurt generally don't want to be hurt again. You may notice a heightened, linguistic response in some of the participants, that not even the slenderest of margin exists between some words and their being acted out. Mention the word 'punch', and some start punching. The power of the situation and the dilemmas of the characters should hold their interest beyond this almost habitual response and provide a solid foundation for the work on dilemmas which follows in Feelings. The discussion of the play and rehearsal different resolutions are also important here. Be sure to allow enough time for both.

A slow closing to this session should ensure that no one is left overenergised when they leave the workshop. If you feel the group still need more centring before they leave you, ask them a few practical questions about their next activity and about where it is to be held.

Workshop Two – Power

Contents

Closing

2.13 One Thing

2.14 Reach for the Stars

Materials

- name badges
- the 'map' of the workshops sessions
- several large sheets of paper, and three marker pens
- the red, the blue and the green colour puppets.

Introduction to the second workshop   5 minutes

Sit on the floor, and, if possible, without verbal command, let the group join you, making a circle. If you are using a multilingual approach, greet them, perhaps in one of the other languages in the group as well as English. Ask the group to remember the workshop they did with you. What was it about? Confirm it was about trust and ask for some feedback on that first workshop. Some of the participants may have been absent and this is a positive way of recapping for everyone. Tell the group this workshop, the second of six, is about power – you may want to use the word in other languages. In introducing the theme of the workshop it is important to show how power fits into the overall structure of the workshop, so that there is an available context for understanding it as part of a process, not as an end in itself. This is done by showing the map of the workshop again, holding it up for everyone to see where in the journey they are and how many sessions remain. Tell the group how long this workshop will run, and explain that, like Trust, it will be made up of exercises, games, stories and acting, all exploring power, feeling power and using power responsibly, that is with trust and care. If there are any questions, answer them before starting, as informatively and clearly as possible. Then, without command and in a spirit of readiness, stand and invite the group do the same.

Warm up   5 minutes

2.1   Electricity

Raise a finger, turn to the participant on your right, draw a quick zigzag in the air, like electric lightening, and say: 'Pass it on'. Once the 'electricity' has gone right round the circle, send it round in the opposite direction. Then ask someone else to start it and pass it on but being very clear before they do, which way round the circle they are going to send the electricity. If this simple communication game goes well, develop it by passing the electricity back and forth across the circle as well as round it in both directions. This agreeable exercise develops concentration through fun as well as encouraging group relatedness. It also raises energy which is often equated with power.

2.2   Shake and Freeze 2

Reprise this exercise from the Trust Workshop (1.1). At whatever age, people enjoy repetition and repeating exercises builds up a vocabulary of action which nourishes a positive group dynamic through shared learning and achievement, however modest.

2.3   Warm Up Faces 2

Repeat from the Trust Workshop (1.2), perhaps developing and exaggerating the faces and the chewing so that they are larger and the letting go of tension greater.

2.4   Breathing 2

Just as in Breathing 1 (1.4), everyone breathes in for a count of three and sighs out. Now tell the group that on the next breath you are going to let the air out in a different way. Breath if for three and yawn the breath out. Now everyone repeats both the sigh and the yawn one more time. The yawning may continue after the exercise. As long as it is real, allow it to happen. Tension, especially muscular and vocal tension, is released when yawning and is a sign that the participant is relaxing.

Power games   15 minutes

2.5   Elephants

This pleasurable game develops relatedness, quick reactions and co-ordination. Stand in the centre of the circle. When you point to someone, he or she uses their arm to make the trunk of an elephant, while the participant on the right holds their left hand up to the side of the elephant's head to make the elephant's right ear, and the one on the left puts their right hand up to make the other ear. This should happen as quickly as the lightening flash of Electricity (2.1) played earlier. Next, point to a different person in the circle, who in turn makes a trunk and whose neighbours make ears and so the process repeats itself. Play as quickly as you can. Then choose someone to come into the centre to take your place. Choose a participant who might benefit from some power.

Often those of us with low or fragile self-esteem find being the centre of attention almost unbearable but in this case it is only for a very short period of time. He or she then leads the game, for a minute at most, or until everyone has had the chance to be trunk and ears at least once. If time allows, chose a third and last participant to go into the centre. Be firm about stopping. Ask who the most powerful person is in this game, eliciting the response that it is the one in the middle. What power does this person have? It is that of choosing people, changing them into elephants, and controlling the timing. Summing up, note how the game shows that control is a form of power, but that one person being powerful doesn't necessarily mean that the group can't have fun. One person being powerful and controlling this game is, in this case, the means to enjoyment.

2.6   Incy and Falloon

This simple movement-based game is not dependent on any language, only on two made-up trigger words: Incy and Falloon. Standing in a circle, everyone turns to face the same way. Walk slowly in one direction, always staying in the circle. When you say 'Incy', everyone makes themselves as small as possible and carries on walking in the smallest way they can. When you say 'Falloon', everyone makes themselves as big as possible and walks big. Vary the rhythm, putting in quick changes and reversing direction. One development is to reverse direction each time: Incy to the left, Falloon to the right. The whole game lasts only a minute or two. Ask which felt more powerful, Incy or Falloon, and why? Fun in itself, this game continues the experience of playfulness and power whilst acknowledging there can be connections between big/small and powerful/powerless. Being a physically big Falloon can make you feel powerful, and there is nothing wrong with this; equally, being a physically small Incy can make you feel less powerful, and that there is nothing wrong with this either. Both conditions belong to everyone at different times, in different roles and situations. Acting them out is proof that powerfulness does not have to be fixed in the size you are, but depends on what you do. For those whose initial responses are macho posturing, the game briefly allows them to show off their bigness and physicality, but it also challenges them to acknowledge their own smallness in a dynamic which constantly changes. For those participants who do not, for whatever reasons, present themselves as powerful, the game alerts them to the possibility of change and growth, whilst allowing them to be as small as they want. The game looks ahead to the brainstorms later in the workshop on the needs of the baby, toddler and nine-year-old by exploring connections between growing physical size and potentially growing feelings of powerfulness.

2.7   Grandma's Footsteps

This game will be known to almost all participants, although sometimes by different names, such as Wolf Behind the Curtain. This is a deliberate choice to give a mixture of familiar and new games, and to show how even old games can offer new possibilities when they are put in a new context. It employs the same pointing gesture, as Elephants (2.4), played earlier. Join in. One person, Grandma, faces the wall while everyone else retreats to the far side of the room and begins to advance. While Grandma's back is turned, the group can move freely. Whenever Grandma turns, everyone freezes; if Grandma sees anyone move, they have to go back to the start. Eventually someone will touch Grandma without being caught, and take over that role. Grandma's word is final. This game, which is about being subject to an authority figure and in this case a family member, has resonance for the overall protective element of the workshops. Only play this game three times. Don't be cajoled into more. This has the effect of not letting any dominant catchers emerge, not boring the cautious, and not rewarding those seeking attention by spectacularly failing to freeze. The reflection here begins to be complex. Again, ask who has power in this game? At first, Grandma is the most powerful but gradually those nearest her power base gain power until they have the most power, and she least, making it clear groups can have power as well as individuals, and that power positions are not fixed. This can feed into later discussion on what happens when someone is not responsible with their power or abuses it, and the rôle a friend or group of friends might have in that situation.

2.8   Yes, Let's

This game is about individual choice in relation to a group and power. To play this game everyone needs to know these two phrases: 'Let's all…' and 'Yes, let's!' Explain that the game is called 'Yes, let's!' You suggest an activity but you must start the sentence with 'Let's all…' For instance, 'Let's all stand up.' Before the group stand, they must reply 'Yes, let's' and then stand. Lead the game yourself until you are sure the mechanics of the game are understood, then tell the group that anyone can suggest anything. If an activity is suggested that is not liked, anyone can change it, so that the group and the individuals in the group are always making the circumstances that are best for them. If playing with deaf and partially deaf participants, make sure you establish a clear visual signal to introduce a new suggestion like waving arms in the air, stamping on the floor to create vibrations. If the group are shy, or their imaginations are stiff, change the activity yourself into interesting ones like 'Let's all mend a car', 'Let's all dive underwater,' 'Let's all sing' or 'Let's all dance!' Look out for the participant who says 'Let's all stop playing this game!' This is the only way of blocking this game. If it happens after some while, it may mean that the group have played it long enough but if it happens near the beginning, intervene and start the game again, acknowledging that that participant has found the powerful autodestruct button of the game, but you want to play it anyway. Another suggestion to look out for is 'Let's all go home', or one which involves everyone leaving the room or doing some thing potentially unsafe. In this case, come in with your own suggestion which will change the group's activity again. Ask the group what happened during the game. Why was it fun? In this game everyone can be powerful. If there is an activity you want to do, you just have to suggest it and you know in advance that everyone will do what you say. If someone suggests something you don't like, you know you can chane it immediately and that everyone will follow. Because of this positive dynamic, it is an energy-raiser and good for getting everyone involved in playing freely.

Relating   40 minutes

2.9   Powerful Statues

At this point, the workshop makes a significant advance as this next exercise involves connecting experience with touch and the crucial distinction between feeling powerful and having power over someone else or others. Remind the group of the Relax Button (1.3). Now they are each to think of a time in their own lives when they felt powerful – perhaps they had won a race, done something difficult for the first time, or simply felt good about themselves. Be clear you are not talking about being aggressive or having beaten or hurt someone else; that is a false sense of power because it is at the expense of someone else. Real power is not having taken power from someone or having power over them. Your partner is to make a statue of when they felt powerful by modelling you but because you are not clay, they must have a careful touch. Push your own Relax Button and relax over. Your partner makes you into their powerful statue. Freeze when the statue is complete. Swap over. Having demonstrated, the group gets into pairs. Even if the numbers are odd, don't join in as it is important that the work is observed. How participants attempt this exercise can offer clues to the larger processes which have modelled their lives. Perhaps one participant resists relaxing and makes their own shape, revealing an unwillingness to be vulnerable which may indicate experiences of having vulnerability exploited. Another participant, being rough in the modelling and breaking the trust their partner is putting in them, might be re-enacting some memory of a breach of trust in their own life. However, don't judge or interpret, just watch. After both partners have made their statues, go round the circle looking at each one. However carefully this exercise is set up, there will probably still be some violent and menacing statues. Explain these are more to do with the expression of being angry than truly powerful. With appropriate intervention, most participants can get a positive experience from doing these unfamiliar activities; but for a significant minority this relatively simple exercise proves very difficult. Finding it so hard to concentrate, sustain and learn, whatever they do achieve should receive encouragement and affirmation.

2.10   A Time When 2

Still in the same pairs, the group sits. Each person has one minute to tell their partner of a time when they felt powerful, then they swap rôles so that the listener becomes the teller and vice versa. Often when some abuse or breach of boundaries has taken place, listening to someone else's experience is difficult, if not almost unbearable because the sense of self is so fragile. This exercise is an excellent way of developing stamina for taking in the experiences of others. Try to avoid saying 'good' and 'bad' power because, although this seems a simple way to define the use and misuse of power, these words don't actually do that. To emphasise this exercise around power being used creatively, give an appropriate example of your own that the participants can empathise with, for instance, learning how to rollerblade. Some pairs may need prompting but most will talk freely. This exercise repeats the structure of A Time When (1.11) from the Trust workshop. After both partners have talked, ask if anyone would like to tell the group what they shared with their partner. Don't press for contributions as choice and the right to be private are paramount. From the stories that are told, draw the group's attention to the creative use of power, of power being used responsibly. If no one volunteers their experience, tell of a time in your own life when you felt powerful in a positive way. Ask if there are any more contributions, thank the group for the work they have done and pass on to the next exercise.

2.11   Brainstorm 1

Show three of the puppets, the Red, Yellow and Blue, and introduce them as being a baby, a young child of four, and an eight-year-old respectively. If you are facilitating on your own, ask an appropriate participant, perhaps a boy, to hold the puppet representing the baby whilst you hold the other two as you introduce the exercise. If you are working with two other adults, divide into the same three groups as before, name each puppet before beginning, and brainstorm what 'our child' needs to grow and to be healthy and happy. If facilitating alone, work with the whole group, taking one puppet and his or her needs at a time. Tell the group they have only five minutes. Acting as scribe, and not offering any suggestions of your own at this point, write all the contributions down on a large piece of paper. The advantage of having the facilitator as scribe is that you can then repeat back the ideas, in the appropriate language, so that everyone can hear them as they get written down. You will also be able to remind the participants to speak one at a time in case they are tumbling over each other with wanting to express themselves. Your writing will make each brainstorm sheet available to and owned by the whole group, replacing any competitive feeling with that of contributing to a collective list, however excitedly, in an orderly way. This clarity can have an importance for those participants who may not be able to articulate a need that they can feel and have not been able to express themselves. Another obvious advantage is that the facilitator's handwriting should be more legible for the report-back stage, when some or all of the participants read out what has been written. This is a profound exercise for every participant, but especially so for those who have survived or are surviving some sort of abuse or neglect. It might be painful for them to look at what babies and children need if they themselves have not experienced these needs being fully met in their own lives. It is important to know what you need even if you haven't got it or had it. Part of sustaining and experiencing abuse can be the denial of this knowledge, which is a loss needing to be mourned. Ultimately, truth, however painful, is part of healing. These brainstorms on the needs of children at different ages are not only about power and powerfulness. By looking at the needs of people younger than themselves, 'children' in the form of puppets owned by the group, named by them and sometimes held by them, the participants can articulate their own needs in a protected way whether those needs are positive ones, such as 'attention' or 'birthdays' or negative ones, such as 'not being hit' or 'learning not to bully'. At the end of the period of writing, each group presents their findings to the whole class in the Listening Corner. This is the first time that the Listening Corner has been a place for the participants to listen to each other. On one level, this learning to listen to each other is as important as drawing out the themes of a child's growing powerfulness, independence and need for carefulness, which the brainstorms exemplify.

2.11   Puppet Play 2: Ralph and Jane

This next stage of the workshop develops the direction of the brainstorm feed-backs. You may notice from the sheets of suggestions and ideas that while the baby's needs are mostly met by parents or carers, many of the eight-year-old's needs are in the area of friends, siblings, school and social relations. The following puppet play takes these facts into account in its presentation of a story of power being abused. A brother persuades his younger sister into playing a game of cops and robbers she doesn't want to play. The game becomes a pretext for bullying and ends in tears.

For the play, the puppets, Ralph, played by the red puppet and Jane by the green, start off resting on the chest, in advocacy mode, facing you, one on each hand. After the play, ask the participants to get in their three groups again to consider the questions that follow at the end of the play's text. There will be a strong urge to retell the story, which is a valid response, often showing the already remarked-on ability of some of the participants to reproduce a play or story with amazing accuracy of language and tone. As one of the underlying concerns of the workshops is the importance of memory, it is always worth spending time recalling the play, or stories, before going on to discuss them.

The play stops short of a solution, ending with Jane fearful, disempowered and wondering what to do, and Ralph afraid she will tell on him and threatening her with more hurt if she does. Ask the participants for their responses to the situation. Ask them how could the situation be made better. You may be surprised by the variety of ideas and their creativity and sophistication. This post-performance discussion is in many respects the most important part of the workshop and their responses should also be written down and shared with the group when the small groups come back into the Listening Corner.

If time allows, rôle-play suggested courses of action or solutions with the participants acting out the protagonists. Do not let the participants use the puppets. This will be a real distraction and the puppets will lose their magic and perhaps be damaged. If you do get to acting the situation out, be sure to allow enough time to do this, and to de-rôle afterwards. There is another story about the misuse of power, Marcia and Tamsin, in Chapter 9 which you might prefer to use or to use as well.

Ralph and Jane

NARRATOR: This is a story about two members of a family: Jane...

(Present puppet.)

...who is eight years old and her brother Ralph...

(Present puppet.)

...who is ten. One day they came home from school. No one was at home and there was nothing on TV. 'Let's play a game', said Jane. 'Cops and robbers', said Ralph. 'I don't like that game', said Jane. 'Do what I say, Jane,' said Ralph, 'Why?' said Jane. 'Because. Because I'm older and bigger that you. Anyway, we played it before', added Ralph, 'and I'll be the police and you be the robber. Starting now' 'You are always the police,' said Jane, 'it's not fair.' 'We'll change over later', said her big brother, but they didn't. They started to play, chasing all over the place…

(The puppets act this out.)

…and at first it was quite fun. Then Ralph caught Jane. 'Gotcha,' he said, and he held her down.

(The puppets act this out.)

'Ow', said Jane, 'get off me!' and she struggled to get free but Ralph caught her by the neck and began to hit her all over.

(The puppets act this out.)

'I'm stronger than you,' he said, 'you can't escape.' 'That hurt,' said Jane, 'stop it you bully!' And she began to cry.

(The puppets separate and Jane cries.)

Ralph left her alone.

(Ralph moves away from her.)

'I was only playing,' he said, 'don't tell on me, will you?'

(He comes closer to her again but does not hit her.)

Jane didn't say anything. She carried on crying.

(The puppet playing Jane rests on the chest of the Narrator while Ralph faces the audience.)

Ralph was thinking: if she tells Mum or Dad, I don't know what will happen. They might be angry with me.

(The puppet playing Ralph rests on the chest of the Narrator while Jane sadly faces the audience.)

Jane was thinking: I wonder what would happen if I told Mum or Dad. Ralph said: 'Promise not to tell or I'll beat you up again.' Jane said nothing.

(The puppets are left with their dilemmas for a moment, then the Narrator takes them off and puts them back into the bag.)

- What happened in this story?
- What is Jane feeling and thinking?
- What is Ralph feeling and thinking?
- Why did Ralph do what he did?
- What could Jane do?
- What could Ralph do?
- Who can help them?
- How?
- What could parents or adults do?
- What do you think would make the situation better?
- Act out what you think should happen next.

Closing   **10 minutes**

2.12   One Thing

Start this penultimate exercise by saying one useful thing that has come out of the workshop for you. It may be about feeling confidence in our own power, the growing feeling of power in the group or an example of how power has been used sensitively or positively in the workshop, or it might be that you have noticed a new awareness in the participants about their relationships with people that have more power than they do. Ask if the participants found something useful in this workshop. If so, see if there is anyone who would like to share that with the rest of the group. Is there anyone else who would like to say anything? Probably time will be up. Don't press for contributions – again, let them come as they will.

2.13   Reach for the Stars

Closings are always important, and need to be marked appropriately. To finish, everyone stands firmly with their feet a foot apart and parallel. Breathe in and now stretch up as high as possible, reaching for the stars. When you have reached as far as you can, stretching up through the spine, very gradually let the arms relax, keeping the body and head tall and straight. Let the group stand for a short period, feeling strong and centred. Remind the group when the next workshop is and where, and then thank them for all their hard work.

CHAPTER 5

Workshop Three: Body

This third workshop, Body, explores the participants' subjective experience of being and having bodies and the connection, often an unconscious one, between the way children and young people are treated because of the age or size of their bodies and how their bodies can react. A significant element of the whole workshop journey is the emphasis on acting out and experience as a means of comprehension to support and complement spoken language as a means of learning. This is the only workshop that requires a significant amount of practical preparation, as the participants make their own 'bodies', and these puppet shapes have to be cut and stapled in readiness for the session.

To begin in an appropriate spirit, the very opening seconds of the workshop are in gestural or body language only. The early part of this workshop recognises that bodies have boundaries and the security and safety of each one of us depends on these boundaries being respected. When boundaries are breached, by abuse or neglect in whatever degree, a profound loss of innocence results and psychological hurt. Emotions, thoughts, and pain too complex or too excruciating to be borne are often buried in the physical body. This is evidenced by stiffness, lack of co-ordination, agitation, numbness, or by over-loose responses. One of the many consequences of suffering or surviving abuse can be the so-called mind/body split, the divorce of conscious process and physical being. Obviously all warm-ups and games are exercises of the body, but they can have different functions and feed into different levels of reflection and learning according to how they are set up, structured and developed. The body is the physical site of self.

The cheerful opening games, such as 'Hello body!' in which the boundaries of the body are greeted and grasped, are designed to create positive energy and the easing of tension. The warm up for this workshop goes on to reprise some by-now familiar exercises, like Relax Button and Breathing while varying them and developing them.

Mirror work is introduced for the first time. Those of us who have not had their actions reflected back to them by positive and consistent parenting, may have an insecure and fluctuating notion of self. Mirror work is a direct and powerful form of acknowledging existence, one's own and another's, as well as creating helpful pair relationships within the whole group. As with all the exercises and games found in the early part of the workshop, they take seconds rather than minutes, but even so they have a remarkable effect in raising levels of energy and concentration, and in reducing inhibitions that are the symptoms of fear of failing or shyness. They also enact a physical centring of the work in the body and offer physical memories for later understanding.

This workshop more than any other asks you, the facilitator, to look at the metaphorical meanings the body carries. For example, it will be plain to see the participant who looks burdened, remote, hectic, off-balanced and so on. Subsequent exercises aim to give the participants a positive picture of themselves and what they need to be healthy and safe, and to identify the difference between stress and relaxation, both mental and physical. The workshop also makes clear that parts of our bodies are private and we have the right not to let ourselves be touched. Whoever we are and at whatever age, if that touch is unwanted, we can say 'no'.

The elephant puppet, Rani, is a catalyst to stimulate consciousness around the body as well as the more obvious rôle of her being a means to articulate difference between human and animal. Through her agency, positive information is elicited about what makes bodies feel good, with the implicit message that some things can make us feel bad about ourselves and our bodies. Rani speaks directly to the group, without going through the agency of a facilitator. This is the most powerful relationship any puppet so far has made with the group, and it is a significant step towards all the puppets being presented with more autonomy, a progression which provides the participants with working examples of empowerment, albeit it through inanimate objects.

The participants now make their own puppets. They could make their own puppet bodies but there is a distinct advantage in everything being available for them, which is not only a time concern. Although the preparations for this require some labour from the facilitators, having everything organised and prepared for the puppet making creates an enthusiasm linked to a raised sense of self-esteem in the group. They feel taken care of and that they have been given permission to be careful yet creative themselves. The paper bodies of the puppets, if this is the method of puppet making you choose, could all happen in a separate yet related session or lesson, if you or the teachers concerned can organise it, but the energy is more immediate and applied more directly if the participants make their puppets now. The making and naming of the puppets transforms the participant into a sort of parent or carer and also furthers the idea of conferred identity.

The stories in this workshop are not followed by discussion. This has been a very busy session and the participants will welcome an opportunity of just being able to listen. The first story, Reading The Koran, shows that the body can be hurt by words. The second story, Nadia's Grandfather, about unwanted touch, is especially suited to the ending of a session since it does not pose a dilemma, but comes to a calm resolution. The long perspective of the story offers the assurance that a person can, with courage, learn from their own negative experience and turn what they have learnt into helping protect someone else in a vulnerable situation or condition. Although in this story it is the grandfather's behaviour which changes, there is another message here: that it is possible for someone to change by making a conscious decision to break a habitual pattern of behaviour. About tickling, the story takes up one of the disputed pleasures of the body from the session's earlier brainstorm, and shows the negative effect it can have, when a young child is powerless to prevent her grandfather from touching her in a way which is unwanted. Both stories bring together the physical and the psychological sides of how bodies hurt, and forge links with the existing themes of power and trust. Finally, what Nadia's Grandfather in particular offers is a story of healing.

As the body, as both physical and as the site of self, has been the sustained focus of the workshop, the de-briefing or closing of the session is perhaps more crucial than ever. In the final exercise, the body is 'warmed down' and the workshop ends in a linguistic and gestural quietness, with the body balanced, poised and brought to a point of shared stillness.

Workshop Three – Body

Contents

Make and meet

Relating

Closing

Materials

- name tags
- the 'map' of the workshop sessions
- several large sheets of paper and three marker pens
- Rani, the elephant puppet and the colour puppets
- the paper puppets' bodies
- a ruler for each participant
- stick-on parts of the puppets' bodies, (optional)
- glue (optional)
- crayons, coloured pencils, and felt tipped pens.

Preparation

From stiff coloured paper, cut two puppet shapes, (see figure 1), for each participant and staple them together at the marked places. The puppets are then ready to be decorated and have rulers inserted into them to become simple but expressive stick puppets. If you feel you have the time, you can cut body parts and decorative shapes out of variously coloured paper to be glued onto the puppet body. This means more sophisticated puppets can be made in a shorter period of time during the actual workshop itself. If you do take this option, be sure to keep the respective shapes in their own trays or containers for speed and clarity, and that each participant has their own glue.

Introduction to the third workshop   2 minutes

Begin by sitting in the circle. Greet the group using body language. Hold your thumbs up in the almost universal gesture of 'okay' but do this with a quizzical expression. See if the group will answer you with their own unequivocal thumbs up. Greet each other in the different languages you have been using and add new expressions. By now confidence about using other languages will have increased and be an established part of beginning each workshop. Ask the group briefly to recall the two previous workshops, using the map of the workshops to locate where they are in the journey and then introduce the theme of this workshop, Body. Use other words from different languages for 'body' before finding out if there are any thoughts or questions. Then begin.

Warm up exercises   **8 minutes**

3.1   Hello, Body!

Standing up, feet hip width apart, the participants follow your example of saying, 'Hello body' as they briskly rub their arms, their hands, their bodies, and then, bending over from the waist, their legs. This quick game gets each participant to acknowledge their body, to feel their body, to feel that their body belongs to them and to feel where it stops and the rest of the world begins. This simple start is of great value in establishing boundaries because in any situation that is in any way abusive, it is boundaries, whether physical, emotional or psychological, that are breached.

3.2   Relax Button 2

By now, this exercise will seem a familiar one, and may have become a favourite. Pay more attention to the unwinding. This needs to be demonstrated so that everyone can get the rhythm of the slow unwinding of the spine back to the vertical. Repeat no more than three times. Notice if any of the more volatile participants have increased their physical concentration. Whatever the developments from the participants, comment on them positively and commend them.

3.3   Breathing 3

Hold up your hand and begin to breathe in deeply, using your fingers to count to three. The group will recognise the breathing exercise and join in. Deepen the benefits of the exercise by improving the technique. To counter the tendency to snatch a breath in the upper chest by raising and therefore tensing the shoulders, put your other hand on your diaphragm to illustrate more clearly the breath being drawn into the body. Breathe in and let the breath out in the big sigh. Breathe in again and let the breath out in a big yawn. Next breathe in and blow the lips away rather like the whinnying noise a horse makes. This should be fun and a small surprise. Repeat all three breathes again, still noticing any tightly held shoulders or necks and encouraging as much relaxation as possible. Often good will and the desire to do well result in locked muscles. Try and get these to release and soften.

3.4 Slow-mo Shake and Freeze

This is a variation of Shake and Freeze (1.1). Start by shaking your hands vigorously with the group following you. Then slow the movements right down. The group will need to watch you intently and sustain their concentration, and not break the visual observation and replication of the movement by giggling or talking. See how slow you can make the movements yet with everyone still holding together. The slower you can make the exercise, the more the participants will enjoy their own skill. Come to a complete stop and pause for a second or two. Then congratulate the participants on their work. Those who live in degrees of disturbance or in complex environments often become anxious when there is a slowing down of pace and little or no sound. Developing stamina in slow motion work can increase intellectual and physical concentration both in the workshops and beyond them.

3.5 Mirrors

The final exercise of the warm up brings the body into focus as the theme for the session, bridging the gap between taking the body for granted and realising it. First demonstrate with a partner. Explain that you are going to look into a mirror and your partner is going to be your reflection. Because these are drama workshops, it is important everyone feel good about themselves and ready to act. Perform one everyday action, such as combing your hair, putting on a jacket, or washing your hands. Do this slowly enough for your partner to follow you. In mirror work, it is essential to maintain eye contact for when the person looking in the mirror looks away his or her reflection will cease to exist for that time and the exercise is fragmented. When you have finished, thank your partner and ask the group to turn to face their neighbour so they can work in pairs. In their pairs, they chose which person is to go first. When the first participant has finished their simple action looking in the mirror, the pairs swap. The whole exercise lasts less than a minute each way. This is a useful and unusual means of communication, but the function of mirroring here is to give the participants a heightened awareness of themselves in space and their own bodies. It also gives a brief and literal reflection of another body's subjective experience: someone else's body is perceived as another 'I' rather than an object in someone else's private and subjective world.

Body talk   15 minutes

3.6   Rani the Elephant

In the Listening Corner, present Rani to the group. To communicate, she
whispers in your ear and you speak for her. She knows what it is like to be an
elephant, but she wants to know what it is like to be a human. So that Rani can
know directly from them, ask the participants what the difference is between
humans and elephants. Expect contributions like: 'We don't use our ears to cool
ourselves, elephants don't eat peanut-butter sandwiches, we hunt elephants but
they don't hunt us' and so on. If the group is hesitant, use some of the above to
start them off. If you are working with another facilitator, they act as scribe and
write the suggestions down on a memory sheet, to be put up on the wall later
with the other workshop materials. Rani's final question is to ask the
participants: 'What do your bodies like doing? What makes your bodies feel
good?' At this point, if you are working with other facilitators, go into the three
groups, and put Rani safely away. If not, put Rani away and stay in one large
group in the Listening Corner.

3.7   Brainstorm 2

Each group has a brainstorm sheet and a limit of three minutes. Ask the group
to think of as many different things their bodies like doing which make their
bodies feel good. Write down every contribution. You will find that there will
be probably no inhibitions and if you are working with younger participants,
you will be writing down such activities as going to the toilet, picking your
nose, burping, having an itchy bottom, along with copious eating, energetic
activity and creature comforts. At the end of the time limit, ask each group to
report back to the others in the Listening Corner, with the participants reading
their group's own lists. Other physical activities, such as being tickled and
boxing may have been suggested, and some will say that they don't make their
bodies feel good. Note the discussion without being judgmental. On the other
hand, most groups will agree that feeling proud, doing something good,
getting prizes, objects that make you happy, memories and holidays count as
things liked directly by their bodies and this is an important link to the material
of the rest of the workshop. Don't allow the feedback to go on longer than
necessary. Give the participants praise for their work.

Make and meet   **20 minutes**

3.7   Making the Puppets

The workshop now takes a big and decisive step forward – the participants are empowered by having their own puppets. Have all the puppet bodies, their stick-on parts and glue if you have decided to use them, rulers, crayons and colouring materials all ready but out of sight. With the participants still in the Listening Corner, tell them that they are now going to make puppets of their own. However, if making the puppets has been part of a special interim session, have the completed puppets ready for each participant but also out of sight. Working with completed puppets will require you to adjust the timing of the workshop, allowing more time for each of the other exercises and stories.

Tell the group that they have just ten minutes to make their own puppet, but everything is prepared for them. The tight time limit helps to concentrate attention, lessening the possibilities of dithering or discord, and lengthening the amount of time remaining in which to use the puppets. Reveal the puppet making materials. Give each participant a puppet body and a ruler, then let them chose their colouring materials and get to work. In the space of ten minutes, each participant will create their own unique working puppet which will often be beautiful and always unique. Tell the group when half the time is up and when they have only two minutes left, so that they all have an opportunity to finish. At the end of the making time, ask them to look at their puppet and decide what to name it, and then write the name of their puppet on its reverse side, or incorporate it into its decoration.

3.9   Meeting the Puppets

The group come and sit in the circle. One by one, the participants introduce their puppet to the others. This recalls the other namings from previous workshops, particularly naming the dragon, and underlines how important naming is in an empowering and owning process. Next, each participant looks at the puppet of their neighbour sitting to their left and says one thing that they like about the body or appearance of his or her puppet. This is to explore the effects of giving and receiving positive messages on the theme of the body. Be sure the participants speak directly to the puppets, and expect compliments such as 'I like your hair', 'I like your eyes' and 'You've got lovely buttons!' In older participants, the simplicity of making these puppets may bring out an innocence, and innocence is protective as its characteristic is not to hurt or to be hurt.

3.10   The Puppets' Plays

With the group still sitting in a circle, look again at the brainstorm sheets. Point out the many activities the group said made their bodies feel good. Now, with puppets, the participants get into pairs. They have five minutes to think of and rehearse a puppet play about one or more of these activities. The play only needs to be short – perhaps a minute or two – but it must be about something which makes the puppets, now that they are being invested with life, feel good and which they like. Unless you have made other arrangements, the brainstorm sheets will probably be monolingual. However, allow the plays to be in any language the participants choose. Also say that their puppets can become different characters if wanted, in the same way as the colour puppets transform into other characters. When time is up, the group return with their puppets to the Listening Corner. If there is time, and some pairs want to, ask to see one or two of the plays. Applaud each play, however brief, while trying to stop the very long ones without the interruption seeming negative. If possible, it is really useful to document these plays on video, or audio tape or even just with still photographs. The whole group will enjoy seeing them at a later date, and this kind of material can be a valuable form of de-briefing as well as adding to the archive of the children's creativity in the workshops. Despite the positive content of the plays and the precautions built into the use of the puppets – their fragility, the making, holding and naming of them – some of the plays may involve or end in aggressive and violent actions which might reflect situations some of the participants have been in themselves. If this is the case, then in metaphorical terms, these participants are passing on their own hurt to the next generation. Be aware of these participants and notice if they can take the opportunities these workshops offer to them to break 'the chain of abuse' by consciously choosing to respond differently, even if this can only be sustained for the length of play or exercise. However small such a move is, it should be welcomed with encouragement and praise. When time is up, collect the puppets, letting the group know you are going to keep the puppets safely. Ask them to keep thinking about their plays and planning them as all the plays will be seen in the next but one session, Communicating.

Relating   15 minutes

3.11   Stories about Words and Touch

Rani, held by you, introduces the following story:

Reading The Koran

RANI: Bodies can get hurt, but sometimes words can hurt us. I've heard this saying, and I expect you have too: 'Stick and stones can hurt my bones, but words can never hurt me.' Well, that is not always true. This story, told to me by a young woman called Mina, is a story about how words can hurt you.

(Rani goes back into the puppet bag and the Narrator presents the yellow puppet as Mina.)

NARRATOR: One day Mina was reading the Koran – it is a holy book – out loud. Mina was reading it in Arabic. She thought she was reading really well until her brother...

(The Narrator presents the red puppet.)

...came up to her and said, 'Oh you can't read properly, can you?' And that really hurt because Mina was happy with what she was doing.

There is no need for comment or discussion on this story as the workshop has been very active so far and the participants will probably be glad to sit and listen. Next, Rani appears again to introduce the next story which again, despite its strong content, needs follow-up discussion, unless you decide to change the workshop structure to include one.

Nadia's Grandfather

RANI: This is a story that was told to me by a friend of mine called Nadia.

(The Narrator presents the green puppet as Nadia.)

She knows I am going to be telling it to you and she's very happy about that.

(Animates puppet.)

Nadia was about nine. She loved doing daring things, like climbing, and running and athletics. She had a brother called Sunny who didn't.

(The Narrator presents the blue puppet as Sunny.)

He liked to be quiet and read. When their Grandfather...

(The Narrator presents the red puppet as Grandfather.)

…came to visit, he would try and get Sunny to play what he called 'boys' games' with him, but Sunny never did, so he turned his attention to Nadia.

(Sunny puppet disappears into the puppet bag.)

He did some things that Nadia didn't like and this is one of them. He would catch Nadia, lift her off the ground, and say each time 'Aha, now I've got you,' and then he would tickle and tickle her. At first, Nadia didn't mind at all, but he wouldn't let her go when she shouted 'Stop!' Her grandfather would catch her and say 'Aha, now I've got you', and then he would tickle and tickle her. 'No, no, stop!' Nadia would shout, but her grandfather would laugh and went on all the more.

(Nadia puppet looks depressed.)

She came to dread his visits, because once he had got her, she could never escape. So when she knew he was coming, she'd try to get away from him. She'd read with Sunny in their bedroom while Grandfather was downstairs with Mummy, or she'd arrange to go out with her friend, Hashi. Something. Anything, so she wouldn't get tickled. And she never told anyone how she felt.

(Grandfather puppet goes and Nadia puppet seems to grow up.)

Many years past and Nadia had a beautiful daughter of her own, called Tanya. Nadia's grandfather was still alive. One day he was going to come to see Nadia and her baby. Before he arrived, Nadia started to feel very worried and depressed, and then she realised what it was: she didn't want him to play with her daughter, and tickle her like he had with her! That's what it was! She started to cry and cry as she remembered how she had hated being tickled. 'I am going to talk to Grandfather about it', she thought, 'I am going to tell him that I don't want him ever to do "Aha, now I've got you", and then tickle Tanya as fiercely as he tickled me.' She was frightened of talking to him. He was an old man. She didn't want to hurt him but she knew that she must talk with him or she wouldn't stop being worried.

(Grandfather puppet reappears.)

When he arrived, they talked, and she told him not to ever tickle Tanya, and how it had felt to her when she was a child. At first, the Grandfather laughed at her, and said he couldn't remember what she was talking about. He said she was imagining things. Nadia told him how she felt again. Then he got sad, and then he became angry. Then he thought about it, and in the end he agreed. He said he would never ever play with Tanya like that.

(Grandfather puppet goes and Rani reappears.)

RANI: Nadia told me:

NADIA: I needed a lot of courage, Rani, to tell my Grandfather about the tickling and I cried a lot, but I felt better and I'm glad I did. It's made things better between my Grandfather and me, but most of all, I know it's best for me and best for Tanya.

RANI: And that's the end of the story Nadia wanted me to tell you.

Closing   5 minutes

Bring the group back into the circle, standing. Ask for any thoughts, ideas, suggestions. Remind them that their puppets will be kept safely by you until the fifth workshop, the one after next, and that as everyone has worked very hard, it is time to warm down our bodies. With the feet parallel and about a foot apart, and explaining the exercise as you do it, stroke your arms as if brushing feathers off them softly, your face, your hair, your body, your legs and your feet. Do this slowly and calmly. Bring the feet together and stand tall with the spine straight but relaxed. Breathe in through the nose with no count at all and let the breath out through the mouth making no sound. There should be a calm concentration in the circle. Stand for a moment or two like this and then thank the participants and remind them when the next workshop will be.

CHAPTER 6

Workshop Four: Feelings

Because of its content and its place in the sequence, this workshop on feelings is perhaps the most dynamic of all the sessions. The participants began their journey with Trust, with which they explored Power and then, in Body, they reflected on themselves, physically and psychologically, having gained some awareness of how trust and power can affect personal safety and self-esteem. It is only at this point that feelings are approached.

Feelings, both emotional and intuitive, happen in us and to us, sometimes in ways and with reasons that we don't fully understand at the time, at least rationally. Feelings are powerful: we need to trust them, and feel them in our bodies. In this workshop the hardest challenge is for you, the facilitator, to explore primary feelings such as anger, jealousy and joy without the participants becoming overwhelmed by the feelings themselves. Those participants who have already endured difficulties may only have a very frail margin between talking and thinking about a feeling and acting on it. For example, someone may talk about punching and almost instantly you may see some participants punching. This workshop's main objective is to give the participants the consciousness that they can and will have strong feelings, like feeling angry enough to break something, but that they can acknowledge those strong feelings without having to act on them or, at the opposite end of the spectrum, repress them to the point of a general numbness which is disguisd despair.

Equally important, a skill this workshop offers is validating feelings that have no name and seemingly no explanation, perhaps a feeling of alarm, of something not being quite right or uncomfortable, perhaps a word, a look or a touch. These feelings are commonly present in situations which have connections to abuse. Abuse is almost always disguised as something else; often as its opposite. Young people's feelings are usually shaped by adults according to the adult's own notions of what is right, unfair, or allowable. Whether they accept or reject these received ways of being, children and young people all too frequently inherit their carers' attitudes and values without being helped or allowed to express their own authentic emotional character.

As adults, we can also influence the feelings of those in our care in another significant way: if we find extreme emotions of any kind daunting and dangerous, we may do our best to avoid them by trying to inhibit or control feelings in ourselves and those around us. Even though modern psychology has taught us more about our makeup, we still repress emotions hoping that by not letting ourselves feel we can and will eliminate the feelings themselves and their cause. What we repress in ourselves we often cannot tolerate in our children or other younger, or less powerful people, but the price of this intolerance is high. We cannot banish what is true for too long without some disjunction or damage to our potential to grow, relate and be creative. We become choked full of feelings that sooner or later feel 'bad' because these feelings are not expressed – or worse, we are made to feel such feelings are bad in themselves, and we are very bad for even having them.

In the careful design of these workshops, by the time this session is reached, an interested confidence and positive group relatedness should exist, which will give the participants enough energy to discern the difference between their feelings and the feelings of others. In other words, the participants will be more intensely aware of themselves, and others, as subject in their respective lives. This understanding brings with it the discovery that everyone is different and has a right to their feelings, although this does not confer on anyone the right to act on every feeling, especially if respect for others and their safety is jeopardised. When abuse takes place the abused person becomes the object of another's desire to control and disempower. Feelings are a sign of being a person and subject in one's own life. The journey from feeling like an object over whom others have power into being the body and centre of your own life is painful, for in order for this to happen the loss of innocence has to be acknowledged and grieved.

The warm up includes new games and exercises, mostly to do with transformation and flexibility, of changing faces, walks and feelings. Being allowed to show the most hideous grimace of rage can be cathartic because the games show implicitly that such large emotions do indeed exist, and second, that we can all feel. Here, in the opening two sections of the workshops, feelings are allowed to be felt just for themselves, independent of story, owner and judgement, and without outcome. Then, when the workshop focuses on powerful emotions, these feelings happen to others, represented by the puppets – in themselves charismatic objects – through the safe catalyst of a story. This does not mean that the participants are being protected from emotion by distance or displacement; rather they are being given a safe and therefore intrinsically creative context in which to empathise, identify and reflect.

The dynamic of dilemma is the subject of the puppet play, *Carlo's Dilemma,* which shows how we feel when our feelings are strong but conflicting or confused. Dilemmas are defined, stated and offered as interactive opportunities for debate and problem solving.

As this workshop draws to a close, debriefing must be given its full time and importance. The participants empty themselves and their faces of all the feelings they have touched on during the workshop. Working together, they raise a huge, imagined mirror and return it carefully to the ground, literally earthing their own experience of Feelings. The last few minutes of this session are for you to check with the group to see if they have any thoughts, responses or questions for you about this or any of the preceding workshops that need your attention. Finally, thank everyone and, as usual, remind them of the time and the place of the next workshop.

Workshop Four – Feelings

Contents:

Materials

- name tags;
- the 'map' of the workshop sessions
- photographs and pictures of feelings (optional)
- circles of cut paper, one for each participant with some spares, and crayons, felt tip pens and coloured pencils
- the colour puppets.

Introduction to the fourth workshop   3 minutes

Greet the group in the way you feel to be the most appropriate. Tell them this fourth session is called Feelings and show the participants its place on the map of the journey. Say that whoever we are, whatever we are, all of us human beings have emotions and emotions are the same in us all, although why we feel what we do is different for every single human being. Ask the participants how they are feeling and reflect back their answers to them, without judgement or comment. Then ask the group if they are ready to start, and begin.

Warm up exercises   15 minutes

4.1   Circle Walks

The participants walk slowly in one direction around the circle. After a few seconds, ask them to walk more quickly. Once this new pace is established, ask them to walk slowly. Then ask the group to imagine they are walking through mud. Let this develop, encouraging them still to move forward round the circle in spite of being 'mud-bound'. Change the direction of walking as you ask the group to move on ice, skating, slipping, sliding. Keep the walk going then step into the centre of the circle yourself, like a lion, and ask the group to walk and move and roar like a lion. It is a good idea to start with the lion – or any of the traditionally aggressive big cats – since at this point the participants are focusing on the walking aspect of the mime. Varying the direction, follow lions with any judicious mix of animals: snakes, chickens, monkeys, kangaroos and so on. The function of this game is that the transformation into animals has a liberating effect. By changing their bodies into different shapes – with a different feel to them – the group feel able to express feelings more freely.

Stop walking, and get and give some brief responses to the circle walks so far. Following on immediately from the animal walk, change the direction of movement of the circle, and give and demonstrate instructions to walk in a sad, angry, frightened, happy way. Each feeling lasts no more than a few seconds.

Setting up the exercise as a walking one is an excellent way of letting the participants approach feelings safely and energetically.

4.2   Shaking All Over

The group, still in their circle, stand with their feet parallel and their spines straight. Ask them to press their 'relax button' so that they relax over from the waist and then ask them to stay there and not come up to standing. Join in yourself, giving the instructions for the exercise as you demonstrate. Then, with the weight of the body still hanging over, shake the arms, the head, and the shoulders. Shake yourself to an upright position, coming up gently through the spine. Stand on one leg and shake the other foot, and repeat standing on the other leg. Put energy into the shakes. Shake vigorously. Then add voice. Shake the voice out of you. It will sound like a deep, sustained 'ah'. Most probably, the participants will laugh at the unstructured sound but keep going – the exercise only lasts a few seconds anyway – until everyone overcomes their self-consciousness, and joins in, enjoying the freedom of letting go of the voices.

4.3   Waking Up Faces

Now lightly massage your face with both your hands, saying to the participants that it is time to wake up the faces, to make them very ready for the acting they are going to do. Rub the temples and the forehead. Stroke the cheeks and the jaw muscles. Warm up the upper lip and the chin. Stretch open the mouth very wide, then contract it as much as you can and then blow the lips away, very much like the horse sound the participants already know from the Breathing exercise. Pick up on any extreme face made by the group and commend them for their expressiveness.

4.4   Breathing 4

Prepare the group for this next exercise by letting them know that they are going to add another breath to the sequence. Stand well. Again using the fingers, count up to three. Breathe in without tension and without straining in the shoulders or upper spine. By now, the participants will be very willing to breathe in and let the breath out in the sequence they have already learnt: a sigh; a yawn; and a horse noise. Now, as you expel the fourth breath, use it to cry with, uninhibitedly, like a baby. When the fourth breath and its crying is spent, come to stillness. This is the first point in the workshop where an emotion is directly expressed, albeit it in a primary and abstract way. Don't let the participants get carried away and embark on long spells of crying, however fake or amusing. As soon as the breath is finished and the next breath is caught, swiftly continue on to the following exercise of the warm up.

4.5 Up And Down Faces

Standing in the circle still, and, if possible, without using words to explain, raise one hand horizontally, palm towards you, up to your face. Lower it slowly, revealing a smile. Now raise the palm, leaving a sad frown behind. Repeat, getting the group to join in the exercise too. Again this game doesn't last too long, just enough time for everyone to do it. Circle Walks has located feelings in the body, using the whole body in motion; this exercise brings the energy more consciously to the face, allowing control and exchange. This game practises happy faces and sad faces, but above all it enacts the changing of faces. Sometimes, as a result of a numbing experience, a face can become a mask: features are frozen, feelings don't register, the face acts as a survival shield. Any participants wearing masks can feel that this is a chance, with you, to change and move their faces and feelings. It is also revealing, when the ups and downs are all done rhythmically together, to see the effect that everyone's smiling or frowning has on each individual. End with a smiling face.

4.6 Throwing Faces

This next circle game picks up on this communicative side of making faces, and concentrates the focus further, this time onto individual faces. Make a face – extending the range of emotions already manifested by choosing another one, such as 'surprise'. Freeze that face in an appropriately surprised expression, then gather it with your hand as if you are taking off a soft cloth mask, and prepare to throw it to someone else across the circle. This may need to be one of the more confident members of the group who will not mind being involved in this tiny improvised moment. Tell the participant to catch it, put it on, and then change the face to one of their own. Throw the face. The participant catches it in their hand, puts it on like a mask, looks 'surprised' for a moment, and then changes it to a feeling of their own, for instance, 'happy'. They then throw their 'happy' face to someone else, and the game continues, if possible until everyone has had a go. It doesn't matter if faces are repeated; invariably they will be since some of the participants will not be confident enough to invent a feeling of their own or will simply want to try a certain expression that has impressed them. The aim is now not so much to extend the range of feelings but to practice their communication. In this game communication becomes a sort of long-distance mirror work or moulding: getting the message is a question of accepting someone's offered face. By implication this means understanding their feeling. This is the most absorbing of the feelings warm-up games, partly because technically it is the most demanding of concentration, but also because it takes up a participant's own individual emotional contribution. This may be a real feeling that the preceding games have generated, or an underlying feeling, which they have released. The releasing does not have to be language based: a feeling may have a name which everyone can identify, but it may not. In either case, the individual contributes it to the game knowing that another peson can and will accept it. Don't hurry this game, but equally, don't be cajoled into playing it for too long.

Feeling feelings   15 minutes

4.7   Feeling Faces

Sitting down for the first time in this workshop, explain to the group that you are going to show them some feelings, and they can recognise what they are. Let your face express any clear, strong feelings in turn: for instance, grief, excitement, fear, doubt, boredom, joy. After each one, see if the participants can identify which emotion you are presenting and then go on to the next emotion. If you know or can learn any sign language, use the signs for feelings: kinetic languages are much more expressive than words in themselves can ever be because the signs have physical connections with the body – for instance, anger and fear come from the heart while anxiety is made close to the head – as well as integral facial expressions. They thus bring together the work of the warm-ups, both expressing and naming feelings. Use words for feelings from other languages either spoken by the participants or being learnt by the participants, emphasising again, more powerfully than any explanation can, that whoever we are, and whatever language we speak, we all feel the same emotions. You may feel in your preparations for this workshop that you cannot express these feelings on your face. Look in a mirror and try. If you can take the risk, it will be of enormous value to the group. If you can act and present these feelings, you will empower the group with a greater feeling of confidence and security. If you really feel you cannot use your face freely enough to express these feelings, find photographs from newspapers or magazines of real people and use them instead. Do not neglect to sit down for this exercise. Being on the ground gives you and the participants the experience of being earthed; even in simple exercises like these, the contemplation and exploration of emotions has a powerful effect and it is sensible to be well grounded.

4.8 Feeling Faces 2

As a culmination of all this exploration and learning, the participants next draw feelings of their choice on circles of paper. Have pencils and crayons handy. Take a circle of paper, and demonstrate how with a few strokes of the crayon the eyes, nose, mouth and eyebrows of a 'feeling face' can be drawn. Give the participants a paper circle each and pens, and tell them they have a time limit of one minute only to draw a feeling face of their own. After everyone has finished, go round the circle with everyone in turn holding up their feeling face. Reversing the process of the previous exercise, you now see if you can recognise what feeling the participant is showing you, letting the rest of the group contribute too, if they want to which they almost certainly will. If you are unclear about one of the faces, ask what the feeling is. Then collect the faces and display them at the side of the room. The aim of all these warm up exercises is to establish an ethos of having, owning, naming, expressing, sharing, accepting and communicating feelings. In life, things can happen so quickly that understanding takes place only in retrospect, which is particularly true of the expression of feelings. These simple games and exercises are a playful chance for the participants to approach the very complex processes of emotion safely and for only tiny periods of time, thus providing a space for release, learning and reflection.

4.9 Mirrors 2: Feelings

Ask the group to stand and work with the person standing next to them. Remind them of the mirror work that they did in Body. In their pairs, they decide who is to look into the mirror first and lead the exercise and who is to follow and be the reflection. Demonstrate with a partner and lead the mirror exercise. Perform one ordinary action, just as before, but this time, do it with one of the feelings you have been working on; for example, brush your hair very sadly, or put on a jacket happily. Ask the participant you have been working with to identify the feeling if they can. Give positive affirmation to your partner, and then ask the group to do the exercise, adding that after the first person has led the exercise, the pairs will swap roles. Watch the exercise being performed very carefully. Although the actions with emotions might be diffidently or excessively expressed, all deserve praise. This is particularly the case when you see participants that have been shy previously start to take risks, or when you see participants you know can be overly exuberant taking pains to put on an overcoat sadly. Such changes are also a marker that the group dynamic is harmonising and a credit to both you and the participants. If there is time, see one or two of the pairs' work. You may feel it is safer to chose those who you think will be successful performing in front of the whole group as less assured participants can feel exposed, resulting in a small but crucial loss of confidence. Go with your own feelings – playing safe or taking a risk – it's your choice.

Relating   30 minutes

4.10   Stories about Feelings

These two stories, shown one after the other to the whole group, are based on true stories in which understanding about feelings eventually follows after painful and disturbing experiences. Go to the Listening Corner and introduce Mina's Kitten, a story about how you have a right to your feelings, even when someone tries to say they don't exist or don't matter. Dietch And Mr. Ferris is about how telling someone how you feel can help you and how listening to and trusting your own feelings can protect you. If you are facilitating the group on your own you may prefer to use just one of these stories, or to tell a story of your own which relates to the same emotional context, but which will be even more resonant because it is your story. You can speak directly in the discussion about how you did feel then and how you feel now. This is the power of working subjectively, using your own experience.

After telling the stories, divide into the three small groups to discuss them. By now the groups will be firmly established and can incorporate participants who may have missed previous sessions. It is imperative that all the participants have the same input and the chance to discuss the stories or parts of stories they found particularly important themselves. The process of talking about the stories will be one of retelling, saying how you think the characters were feeling at the beginning, crisis and end of the story, and drawing out any messages or lessons that you and the group find in the story.

The advantage of stories is that all the participants can draw out messages that are relevant for them, and they can have their own perspective. The messages from the stories could be of indignation, for example: Mina's cousin shouldn't have put the cat out; of advice: tell someone if a touch feels uncomfortable; of judgement: Mina had a right to hit and scream; or conclusion: your feelings are your feelings, and they are not right, not wrong. The situations in the stories can then be looked at again in terms of what would have been a better outcome, what you would have done or liked to have done. In any case there will be a lot to talk about. With still five minutes left for this part of the workshop, bring the whole group back together in the Listening Corner to report back on each group's responses. It is valuable to record these either on tape or by writing them down. Reviewing them at the end of the session or at a later date, you may well be struck by the sensitivity and sophistication of the participants' contributions.

Mina's Kitten

NARRATOR: Everyone has feelings and everyone has a right to their feelings but sometimes some people say differently. And they can tell you that your feelings don't exist, that they don't matter, and this is what happens in this story. It's a true story, and it happened to a girl called Mina when she was nine years old.

(The Narrator presents the Green puppet to represent Mina.)

Everyday, after school, Mina would go down to the corner shop to play with the shopkeeper's cats. She loved cats. And the shopkeeper promised her when the cat had its kittens he would give her one. She was so happy. And one day, the cat had kittens, and the shopkeeper, as he promised, gave her one. And Mina was so happy she just took the kitten, and without telling her Mum she'd taken it, she took it home. She pleaded: 'Please, Mum, let me keep it, let me keep it!' So her Mum let her keep it. Her brother didn't like it and he was frightened of it, and her cousin, who was older than her Mum, hated it because the kitten messed around all over the house and was very untidy. Mina was the only one who loved it.

(The Narrator presents the Red puppet to represent the cousin.)

One day, the cousin came down and said to Mina, 'Would you like to go for a ride?'

And Mina said, 'Oh yes, please.'

The cousin said, 'Bring the kitten with you.'

And Mina got the kitten, and got into the car and went for a ride. It seemed like a long way away, but now I know it was only two streets away. Mina's cousin stopped the car and said,

'Let me have your kitten.'

And she gave it to him. And then he opened the door of the car and he let the kitten go.

Mina said, 'What are you doing? What are you doing to my kitten?'

And he goes, 'Let her go here. She's got more space to play in now.'

And Mina says, 'Why are you doing that?'

And she started screaming and shouting and kicking him, and she started crying.

She said, 'Why are you letting my kitten go? I'll never see it again.'

And he goes, 'It doesn't matter.'

And he took her home. Mina was crying all the way home. When she got home she cried and cried and told her Mum what had happened. And her cousin said,

'What are you crying for? It's just a cat. There's no need to cry. Why are you so upset for a cat? It's just a kitten. There's no need to cry.'

And Mina was so upset she went, 'Oh Mummy Mummy, why did he do that?' And her mum did not know anything about it and she was very angry with her cousin.

Dietch and Mr. Ferris

NARRATOR: This is a true story about a boy called Dietch.

(The Narrator presents the Yellow puppet to represent Dietch.)

DIETCH: When I was nine, I started learning French at school. My teacher was Mr. Ferris. In the classroom, he told us that if we were having problems with the work we should go up to his desk and he would help us. One day, I went up to the desk because I was having problems with the work. While he was helping me, he put his arm around me and started touching my bottom and my legs. I didn't know what to do. A few days later, I told my friend Charlie Seymour. He told me that the same thing had happened to him. The more boys I talked to, the more I learned it had happened to them. He was touching all of us. It felt good to know I wasn't on my own, but it still didn't feel right. Because he was doing it to all of us, we all thought that it must be all right, so we never told anyone. That was over twenty years ago and now I know that it wasn't right and now I wish I had told an adult about it. I didn't listen to my own feelings because I thought I was the one who was getting it wrong.

4.11   Puppet Play 3: Carlo's Dilemma   15 minutes

Back in the Listening Corner, introduce the puppet play, by saying it is about a boy called Carlo who is in a dilemma, explaining that a dilemma is when someone feels strongly about something but doesn't know what to do, because one voice inside him is saying one thing, and the other part of him is saying something different. Tell the story using the puppet which states Carlo's dilemma and then ask for two participants. Because a dilemma is when a person has a problem but cannot decide what to do, position the two participants, one on each side of Carlo to take the roles of contradictory inner voices. Each advises taking a different course of action and is as persuasive as possible. The aim here is to open up the space between someone's experiencing a strong feeling, in this case anger, and their acting it out, in this case telling rather than hitting out. Implicit in the technique is that having conflicting 'voices' in one's head is normal, and that negotiation between them is possible, and similarly in everyday life too, talk, dialogue and negotiation are processes for solving problems or resolving dilemmas. You may well want to use a different dilemma from the one given here, one which is more pertinent to your particular participants. Be sure if this is the case that you as the facilitator have a resolution which you will give when the dialogue between the two conflicting voices has been fully explored. What this dilemma work shows in terms of feelings is that having a feeling is one thing – and an inevitable, incontrovertible thing – but how you negotiate with your inner voices and inner urges is the key to how you act on that feeling and relate with other people.

Carlo's Dilemma

NARRATOR: This is a story about a boy called Carlo.

(The Narrator presents the Blue puppet to represent Carlo.)

CARLO: My name is Carlo. This is a story about when I had some very strong feelings and I was in a dilemma. A dilemma is when you can't decide what to do. One part of you wants to do one thing and another part of you wants to do another. In this story I didn't know what to do. It happened when we were on a school journey at a house on a farm. My best friend was called Yanni.

We did everything together – schoolwork, football, swimming. But there was another boy he was friendly with, called Hugo. On the coach I sat next to Yanni. On the way we were telling each other things and I said: 'I hope the teacher leaves the light on in the room tonight.' 'Why?' asked Yanni. 'Because at home I always sleep with the light on – I'm afraid of the dark.' 'Me too,' said Yanni. 'I'm also afraid of the dark.' Later that night, when we were all in bed, the teacher came in and said: 'I'm going to switch off the light now.' Yanni said: 'Leave it on. Carlo is afraid of the dark.' The teacher left the light on. All the others in the room started to tease me and call me: 'Scaredy cat, scaredy cat.' In the morning, at breakfast, Yanni walked straight past me and went to sit with Hugo. I saw them whispering together. I was so angry I just stood there. I felt like my body was on fire. I felt torn in two. I didn't know what to do. It was like there were two voices inside me: one of them saying, 'Hit him. Your friend has betrayed you. You want to kill him,' the other voice saying 'Of course you are angry but hitting him won't do any good.'

NARRATOR: That was Carlo's dilemma: what to do with his anger at his friend betraying him.

(The two participants who are to take the conflicting voices now stand at each shoulder of the puppet representing Carlo and each makes their case. For example:)

PARTICIPANT ONE: Yanni has broken your trust. He deserves to be hit. Smash his in.

PARTICIPANT TWO: Take it easy. You'll be more powerful if you ignore him. He's more afraid than you are. That's why he can't face talking with you.

PARTICIPANT ONE: He embarrassed you in front of your friends.

PARTICIPANT TWO: Just because you're angry doesn't mean you have to hurt someone.

PARTICIPANT ONE:	You'll feel better if you hit him.
PARTICIPANT TWO:	You'll feel even better than that if you go and tell him how you feel. Remember he is more scared than you are. He's already told one lie. If he's a liar do you want him for a friend?

(Thank the voices and ask them to stop their dialogue in order to resolve the dilemma.)

NARRATOR:	In the end Carlo did get up his courage and go and talk to Yanni. Carlo told him exactly what he thought about what he'd done. But they didn't stay friends. Carlo found someone else to trust and with whom to be friends.

Closing   12 minutes

4.12 Stroking Faces

Come back into the circle with the participants standing facing the centre. Just as the faces were warmed up at the beginning of the workshop, now, more slowly, stroke the faces again, taking off feelings from the face and from the body as if brushing feathers softly from the body. There is no great need for words.

4.13 Mirrors 3: A Giant Mirror

Simply say that now, to close this workshop, imagine that there is an enormous mirror lying on the ground filling the whole circle and that you and the whole group are going to pick it up and lift it carefully a little way off the ground and replace it just as carefully. As you ask the participants to join in, bend down and grasp the edge of this mirror. Together, with great care, lift the imaginary mirror up, keeping the group together. Judge how far the group can sustain this group concentration and mime. Probably, the mirror will lift only a small distance from the ground. This difficult collective act using an imaginary mirror reflects and contains the volatile nature of emotions and the challenge and reward of working on and around them. Give positive affirmation to the whole group for their contribution to this important session.

4.14 Checking Out

After the formal finishing of the work of the session, check with the participants if they have any questions, thoughts, or responses they would like you to deal with or answer. As is customary now, tell the participants of the place and the time for the next workshop, and remind them that there are just two more sessions left in this process or journey.

CHAPTER 7

Workshop Five: Communicating

Communicating is a defining feature of relationships. This workshop, the most crucial to safety, looks at the means of communicating and what is or is not to be communicated. In a practical sense all these workshops are about communicating. The circumstances we need for communicating confidently are examined in Trust; Power looks at extending ways of communicating. In Body the ways in which we communicate are articulated, and in Feelings that emotional energy that is nearly always responsible for any kind of communication is identified, and found to be present even when feelings are repressed. In Communicating, the focus is, once again, on content as well as form. The theme of this workshop is not only about ways of communicating, but whether to communicate at all: in other words, it has as its main focus secrets, telling and listening. Overall, you will find at the end of the workshop sequences that there has been a general improvement in communication, both between the participants and between the group and its facilitators.

At this point in the workshop sequence you might like to reflect on how you and the participants, both as a group and as individuals, are communicating – which, of course, is a reflection on your relationships with each other. Have they changed? If so, how? Has the group dynamic shifted? You may have noticed by now that participants who at first seemed to want to be in the background are relating more, with less shyness. Some will switch off during particular puppet plays; some will joke around and cause little vortices of disturbance; others will sit there agog. Have the participants who were desperate for attention calmed down? Have the quiet individuals become more vocal or self-confident? Has your attitude towards any of the participants changed or been changed by any part of the workshop process? Has there been any improvement in language acquisition? What is happening to this group outside the sessions? Give yourself time to think about some of these issues.

Although it is easy to want to interpret behaviour, try only to observe. Your own documentation will be invaluable. What, if anything, is impeding communication between you and the group? Shyness is one possibility, as is displacement behaviour – when some participants react in unconsciously negative ways to input which they can't cope with, and so are disruptive, giggly or withdraw into a private world. But withdrawal and non-participation themselves need to be understood as forms of communication.

Good communication requires trust. Communicating, as the early brainstorm of the workshop will reveal, is about more than just spoken language. If sign language is one of the languages you are working in, naming the workshop by using the sign for 'communication' can take on an emblematic quality. The sign consists of two letter C's made by each hand, moving alternately from and towards the signer's body. The sign emphasises the two essential qualities of communication: that it is a two-way process, and second, it is not made only with the voice, or hearing, or any one of the senses, but it is a marker of being human. The reciprocal nature of communication is demonstrated throughout the workshop, especially in the puppet plays, and then in the preparations for the participants' own puppet plays.

The early part of the workshop concentrates on raising awareness around listening skills, such as noticing body language, eye contact, and giving attention. The warm up games are not only designed to go on freeing the body but also the voice in psychological preparation for the immediacy of using volume; for example, of shouting 'no', of speaking up for oneself, of breaking the silence of secrets, and of shouting for help and support if this is necessary.

A playful anarchic energy will be generated by the games and exercises of this workshop in which authority, when linked to misleading information, is challenged and subverted. This experience, lodged in games and exercises which are fun and funny, will help the participants to detect the difference between an actual fact and its distortion through wrongful naming or commands: whatever the name, the fact or act remain the same.

Next there follow some short puppet plays on the complex issues associated with communication and safety. These plays are more distinctly theatrical than before, and are deliberately given certain formal characteristics, such as entrances and exits, locations and punch lines. The workshop asks you, if possible, to set up the simplest of performing spaces in which the puppets can appear. For the first time the puppets can then appear without the protection and ownership of any of the facilitators. This is also the first time the puppets appear in their own right, not playing roles, but themselves. They are not enacting someone else's story but related to each other, independent of their advocates. Both of these moves towards autonomy have great significance in terms of the content of these plays about secrets and telling. A stage of some sort, perhaps made only of a table and screen, will help the puppets to make their relationship with the audience communicative and provocative within the protection of story, imagination and dialogue.

A prologue introduces the theme of the plays: secrets. After each short play one of the animal puppets points out the moral with the traditional phrase: 'Which only goes to show that…' The final play also employs the dynamic of audience participation: as part of the surprise for Blue's birthday, all the audience, as well as the other puppets, are to sing 'Happy Birthday'.

All these conventions are used to give weight to, and make as accessible, open and public as possible, the content of the plays – secrets. Their message is not that keeping secrets is always bad or always good – the plays present a complex enough range of situations to refute this – but that talking about secrets is not itself forbidden; that secrets, telling, keeping and communicating, especially communicating feelings, are issues of crucial importance to everyone.

You will choose and adapt the plays as necessary according to your own situation and circumstances. However, these ten plays have been written out of consideration for the special requirements of participants who may be survivors of still-secret abuse, and deal with the reality of secrets in terms of messages. This concern led to the following morals for the stories, but it may be that only some are appropriate to your own use or that you will want to devise others:

- secrets sometimes give you power over others
- it's all right to keep some things to yourself – you don't have to give everything away
- if by keeping a secret you are hurting someone (including yourself) it is all right to tell
- if someone is hurting your friend and you know about it, it's OK to tell
- sometimes keeping a secret can hurt you
- sometimes you have a secret you just have to tell because you are bursting to share it with someone
- making a secret with someone involves trusting them to keep it
- if someone is hurting you but tells you to keep it secret it is OK to tell someone else, someone you trust
- it's all right to wait until you are ready to tell a secret

- some secrets designed to give someone a surprise, for example, a birthday party, and are positive and good.

The later part of the workshop continues to underline the two-way nature of communication: the participants have listened to the puppets and now it is the participants' turn to start to make their own plays. The decision to begin devising the participants' puppet plays in this session was a deliberate one to improve the group's confidence in future process. Holding on to something and being careful with it for the future supports being optimistic that the future can happen and even be imagined, a quality which is of key importance in good self-esteem and in feeling safe. The participants' plays will enact and further the content of this workshop's stories about telling and not telling, knowing and trusting when you feel ready to do something, and choosing the right moment for communicating. If there has been some abusive experience or breach of boundaries, imagining yourself and your actions in the future can be very difficult: it is an act of trust not based on the experience of trust. These plays by the participants are a natural extension of the urge to communicate, particularly as some of the participants may have forged a strong identification with some of the situations represented in these tiny plays and may urgently want to communicate stories and dilemmas out of their own imagination and life through their own creativity. If you are able to work with the participants between workshop sessions, you may want to give them further opportunities to develop their plays.

Workshop Five – Communicating

Contents

Relating

5.10 Puppet Plays 4–13: Ten Plays about Secrets and When to Keep Them

Puppet Play 4: I'm Not Telling You

Puppet Play 5: This Is For Me

Puppet Play 6: It's Okay To Tell

Puppet Play 7: Your Dinner Money Or Else!

Puppet Play 8: I Want To Tell But...

Puppet Play 9: I Can't Keep It Secret!

Puppet Play 10: Don't Tell On Me

Puppet Play 11: Do You Believe Me?

Puppet Play 12: Tell You Later

Puppet Play 13: It's A Secret

5.11 A Puppet Play Of Your Own

Closing

5.12 Tipping The Wink

Materials

- name tags
- the map of the workshop sessions
- large sheets of paper and markers
- the participants' puppets with their rulers
- the colour puppets and elephant and dragon puppets
- a puppet stage (optional).

Introduction to the fifth workshop 5 minutes

Greet the group in the Listening Corner, with the customary languages and ways of welcoming. The opening moments of this workshop are, as usual, a brief recap of previous work, naming of the workshop, and a look at its place in the process. When you tell the group that this workshop, the second to last, is about communicating, make it clear you are not talking about technological ways of communicating, like, for instance, by satellite or through computers, but communicating between us, between people, however it takes place. Ask what communicating is. Reflect back the individual answers to the group by repeating them, and, only if necessary, by commenting on these definitions. Go on to point out that as well as knowing what communicating is, and what and when and where we want to communicate, there is something else, and that is whether to communicate. Some of the stories will be about that later in the session and also about what stops us from communicating.

5.1   Brainstorm 3

Begin the session by getting a large piece of paper and a pen. Tell the group that they have a minute to think of all the different ways we have communicated in these workshops and all the other ways we can communicate. When you give the signal to start, the participants are to suggest as many ways as they can think of to communicate which you will write down on the brainstorming sheet. Be strict. When a minute is up, finish. If there are ways of communicating which have not been mentioned, add them to the sheet as you and the group look at the contributions. Some of the ways of communicating you will find being suggested are: language, writing, drawing pictures, touch, smell, thoughts (for example, telepathy and seeing and talking to others in your imagination), feelings, body language and gestures, dance, music and song. You might want to add that in some cultures people believe they can communicate with others in and through dreams.

Warm up exercises   10 minutes

5.2   Shaking All Over 2

This is a reprise of the same exercise in Feelings, but with the emphasis still more on freeing the voice. By now, everyone's body will be used to being shaken free and relaxing over. See if the same freedom can inform the voices. This is particularly crucial in this workshop, as helping the participants find and strengthen their voices is part of trying to give them effective means to protect themselves, should they be needed. As you lead the group in the energetic yet relaxed shakes, let the sound be shaken out of the body. Free the shoulders, letting the head hang loosely with the mouth and jaw open to let the sound escape without effort.

5.3   Breathing 5

In this session, the sequence of breaths, begun in Trust, is completed. Breathe in for three, marking the count on the fingers, and continuing to check for tensions, particularly in the upper chest, and breathe out first sighing, then with a yawn, then blowing the lips away in a sort of horse sound, then letting the breath out crying and for the fifth and last breath, let the breath out on a laugh. Let the laugh come from the diaphragm in a good belly laugh. Even if nothing is funny, sometimes laughing technically like this can actually trigger genuine laughter. Watch that this does not turn into uncontrolled giggles, however much fun that might be! The group should be coming together well through breathing. Awareness of breath makes voices strong which is important when and if we ever need to speak out or to be heard and whenever we need to communicate.

5.4   AEIOU

All our emotions are expressed in language through the vowel sounds, whereas our thoughts are articulated by consonants. If you consider the last exercise, all crying and all laughing is done with and through vowels. Here, in this next exercise, the participants stand facing each other in a circle. To demonstrate and get the exercise going, move into the centre of the circle yourself, and using the first vowel in the English alphabet, A, use the sound in a specific way. Perhaps you might want to sing it out gladly, or whisper it cautiously, or repeat it quickly like a machine. Make a choice and do it. Whatever you do, the group watches and then repeats. They must repeat the sound and the movement as accurately as they can. Then try another vowel sound, E, still with yourself leading. When you feel confident that the group have grasped the exercise, which is an energy raiser. After three turns, the participant next to you goes into the circle with their own sound and movement which the group will repeat. Spend a couple of minutes on this game. Don't worry if some of the participants get stuck. Let them pass if they don't want to have a turn. Point out this a very simple form of communicating. One person does something in a particular way and everyone else echoes it back. The actual communication isn't changed at all, just reflected. This came is fun and, once it has got underway, will further bring the group together to encourage them to use their voices in an assertive and expressive way.

Getting through   15 minutes

5.5   Yes! No!

Divide the circle into two lines that face each other, with the participants making eye contact with each other. Time this exercise carefully. For fifteen seconds only, one line looks into their partner's eyes opposite and says 'No!' continuously, while the other line, at the same time, does the same but saying 'Yes!'. After the period of fifteen seconds is up, change the positive to the negative so the line that was refusing is now affirming and vice versa. Give them fifteen seconds to interrelate as before. After both sides have tried 'yes!' and 'no!' ask them how they felt. Did saying 'no' make them feel different to when they were saying 'yes'? In reflecting on the exercise, notice how volume was used and body language. The participants may say that they felt angry when they said 'no!' and frustrated when they said 'yes!' but they may also surprise you with their answers, for instance, by feeling calmer and calmer the more they had to uphold their specific position in opposition to another. Play this game only briefly, so that there is no opportunity for any aggression or frustration to build up and make sure none carries over into the rest of the workshop.

5.6   The Floor is the Ceiling!

Tell the participants that in the next game they are to call everything a different name. Start the game off by pointing to the floor and saying very deliberately 'ceiling'. Point to the ceiling and say 'floor'. Then ask the group to walk round the room in a circle, calling everything by the wrong name. Anarchic and enjoyable, this game is another energy raiser which will definitely be of interest and fun especially to those with English as their second language. After a minute or two, stop the game. Point to the wall and ask one of the participants what it is called. Pointing to the window, ask another what it is called and so on. Find out different names for the same object. Because information is distorted in abuse situations, the objective of this game is to make clear that although it might be easy to give another name to something, the thing itself stays the same. As a development, next ask two participants to work with you. The first tells the second the 'name' of something in the room. That second learns the name and repeats it. Thank the first participant and get him or her to sit down. Ask another participant to join you. The second participant tells the third what the name is of the object in question. The third participant does not agree and gives its real name. Point out that sometimes people can give us wrong information and this is confusing when we try to communicate and we have the wrong name for things. This is where we have to trust our feelings. If someone tells us something and it doesn't feel right, we have to try and find out if what they say is true or not. Correct information gives us power which is a prerequisite for learning, the subject of the next and last workshop. It is simpler to play this game only in English, or the language more commonly spoken by the participants.

5.7   Opposites

This game continues the contrariness of the previous game. The group sits on the floor in a circle. The only rule that they must obey is that they are to do exactly the opposite of what you say. Then tell them to sit down. They will stand up. Then you could tell them to be quiet. They will talk. 'Stop laughing!' and they will laugh. As the group grasp the idea of the game, make the commands more complex, like 'Stop making that cake!' This game will also raise energy because it too is anarchic. It puts authority – in this case, your authority as you are facilitating the group – in a different light through the change of power. These exercises and games prepare the participants for this workshop's puppet plays where the imperative to keep secrets is scrutinised and appropriate circumstances in which telling and breaking silence can take place are examined.

5.8   Pass It On

Sitting on the floor again in a circle, tell the group that you are going to whisper a sentence in your neighbour's ear as quietly but as clearly as you can. That person whispers it in his or her neighbour's ear and it will be passed on round the circle. The last person to get the information says the sentence out loud. Ask everyone to try and make sure the sentence remains the same so that at the end, it is the same as it was when it first started round the circle. Play this once, and see how much or how little distortion there is. If the message remains very close to its original, praise the group for communicating well. If there is time, play it again with the last person thinking of another sentence, passing it on round the circle in the opposite direction. If you are working with a large group and facilitating with someone else or as part of a team, play this in two groups. If you are on your own, divide the circle in half and whisper the same message to each of the groups to pass on.

5.9   Brainstorm 4

Get another large sheet of paper and marker. Ask the participants what can stop us communicating. With a time limit of two minutes, ask the group think of all the ways in which we can be stopped or stop ourselves from communicating. Write down the answers. When time is up, without comment if possible, read the contributions back to the group. If you feel there are significant omissions, mention them and add them to the sheet.

Relating   25 minutes

5.10   Puppet Plays 4–13: Ten Plays About Secrets, and When to Keep Them

Now the group go to the Listening Corner, which you may have prepared in a different and more ambitious way. Perhaps you have set up a sort of puppet theatre made of boxes and screens so that the puppets can be seen independent of you and any other facilitators as puppeteers. This is not essential nor will it affect any of the content of the short plays that follow, only their presentation.

the advantage of a stage, however rudimentary, is that it allows the puppets to appear to have a certain autonomy which parallels that of a young person's development. If you are facilitating the session alone, you will have worked out how many of these short plays you can undertake. Have the colour puppets together with the elephant and the dragon puppets laid out on a table in front of you to allow you to pick them up and change them as easily as possible. You may want to change the 'moral' punch lines from Rani or Shalim for you to say instead as narrator or you may decide to alter the gender of the puppets. All ten short plays are given here, including the brief prologue. If you are working with older participants, or want to approach more serious breaches of personal safety, you may want to use Joey's Call To ChildLine which is in Chapter 9. The puppet show ends with the gift to Blue, the shyest character, of a communal song. To finish, all six puppets can take a curtain call, before returning to their bag. After the plays have been performed, break up into the three small groups to discuss them and any other points or questions the participants might have.

I'm Not Telling You

NARRATOR:	We are going to see some plays performed by the puppets themselves, Red, Blue, Green, Yellow with the help of...
	(Give the elephant and dragon puppet whatever names you have chosen, for instance.)
	Rani and Shalim and these plays are going to be all about...
	(The dragon puppet finishes off the Narrator's sentence.)
DRAGON:	Secrets!
	(The elephant puppet enters and overhears.)
ELEPHANT:	*(to Dragon)* Oh, have you got a secret?
DRAGON:	I might have.
ELEPHANT:	Have you?
DRAGON:	I'm not telling you.
ELEPHANT:	Oh go on, tell me! Tell me!
DRAGON:	No, I'm not telling you if I've got a secret.
ELEPHANT:	Why not?
DRAGON:	Because it's a secret!

NARRATOR: As I was about to say, secrets can sometimes give you power over other people!

This Is for Me

(Blue enters and writes. Yellow enters)

YELLOW: What are you doing, Blue?

BLUE: Writing.

YELLOW: What are you writing?

BLUE: I dunno. I think it's a poem.

YELLOW: What's it about?

BLUE: Why do you want to know?

YELLOW: I just do. Let's see.

BLUE: No.

YELLOW: Go on.

BLUE: I'm not going to.

YELLOW: Why? Is it a secret?

BLUE: No. It's private. This writing is for me. I'm writing down my thoughts. It may end up by being a poem or not. It's not finished yet. When it is, and if it's something I want to share, I will and then, if I think you'd be interested, I'll ask you to read it.

RANI: And the moral is: you don't have to tell everyone everything. Have your own secrets or be private – if you want to.

It's Okay to Tell

SHALIM: *(to the audience)* The place: a classroom. The time: a time when nobody should be in it.

(*Green enters, followed by Red.*)

RED: Green!

GREEN: Oh, you made me jump!

RED: What are you doing here?

GREEN: Can you keep a secret?

RED: I don't know. Try me.

GREEN:	You know Yellow?
RED:	Yes.
GREEN:	And you know what Yellow is like: always wanting attention?
RED:	Yes.
GREEN:	You know she's thinks she's the best?
RED:	Yes.
GREEN:	And that she's getting more and more big headed?
RED:	Yes.
GREEN:	Well, see this sticky glue?
RED:	Yes.
GREEN:	And see that chair – Yellow's chair?
RED:	Yes.
GREEN:	And you know her nice new dress?
RED:	Yes.
GREEN:	I'm going to stick her nice new dress with this sticky glue to her favourite chair!
RED:	Are you?
GREEN:	Yes, but don't tell. It's a secret.
	(Green goes off.)
RED:	*(to the audience)* But I did tell because even if Yellow is big headed, I didn't think that was at all the right thing to do.
SHALIM:	Which only goes to show: if by keeping a secret you are hurting someone, it's okay to tell.

Your Dinner Money or Else

RANI:	*(to the audience)* On Wednesday I saw Blue and Red talking. This is what they said:
	(Blue and Yellow enter.)
RED:	Where are you going?
BLUE:	Nowhere.
RED:	Are you all right?

BLUE:	Yes.
RED:	I'll walk home with you.
BLUE:	No, you won't. Why can't you leave me alone? Why does everyone expect me to be cheerful and laughing all the time, now go away!
RED:	*(to audience)* This wasn't at all like Blue. I was worried so I followed him. I saw him stop at the corner of the playground, look round over his shoulder, and then go into the playground. I crept up behind him. No one saw me. I peeped round the wall, and there was my friend talking to three older children. 'Give me your dinner money,' they said, 'or else!' Blue gave it to them at once. 'See you tomorrow with tomorrow's dinner money – or else!' He nodded. He was shaking, then he ran off. I told Green what I'd seen. Green hates it when other people are made to feel scared so we told Rani and Shalim and they sorted it out. Rani and Shalim knew the children that were doing it. They talked to them, and I tell you, those children never did that again.
RANI:	So: if someone's hurting your friend, it's right to tell.

I Want to Tell But...

RANI:	*(to the audience)* I've known Green since she was a small girl. I've always known her to be friendly, bright and cheerful, but some time ago I noticed she was different, quieter, keeping herself to herself. Look! Here she comes now!
	(Green enters.)
	How are you, Green?
GREEN:	Fine.
RANI:	How is school?
GREEN:	Fine.
RANI:	And your family?
GREEN:	What is this? A quiz game?
RANI:	I was just asking. Is anything wrong?
GREEN:	Everything's fine.
RANI:	You know I am always here if you want to talk.

GREEN:	Oh, Rani, I do but…
RANI:	But what?
GREEN:	I can't tell. I've been told not to tell anyone.
RANI:	Your secret doesn't seem to be making you happy.
GREEN:	It's my Dad. He's lost his job but Mum's told me to keep it a secret. She doesn't want anyone to know. There now I've gone and told you.
RANI:	That's a very big secret. I am sorry about your father. It must be worrying.
GREEN:	Don't tell anyone else, will you?
RANI:	Of course I won't. You can trust me.
GREEN:	It's funny but I feel better now I've told you. It's not Dad's fault.
RANI:	No.
GREEN:	And he's got an interview next Monday. So…
RANI:	Everything will be fine.
GREEN:	Yes.
	(Green goes off.)
RANI:	*(to the audience)* Which only goes to show sometimes keeping a secret can hurt you. Oh yes, and by the way, Green's dad did get that job, and Green started to smile again.

I Can't Keep It Secret!

Green is discovered. Yellow enters.

YELLOW:	Could you just listen for a second? Please, please; I want to tell you something.
GREEN:	What?
YELLOW:	But first you must promise not to tell anyone.
GREEN:	OK, I promise.
YELLOW:	Well I think Rani is organising a trip to the seaside for us, but I'm not supposed to know – it's a surprise!
GREEN:	Oh!

YELLOW:	So you mustn't say a word. OK?
GREEN:	OK. I won't. It means I get to use my bucket and spade again!

(Green cheers.)

YELLOW:	Which only goes to show sometimes you just can't keep a secret because you are bursting to share it with someone.

(Green and Yellow cheer excitedly and exit.)

Don't Tell on Me

RED:	Oh Yellow, can I trust you to keep a secret?
YELLOW:	Yes of course. What is it?
RED:	Well, I borrowed Rani's chocolate while she was out. I didn't mean to but I ate it all – I mean, I borrowed it all. I've bought a bar exactly the same from the shop and I am going to put that one where the other one used to be.
YELLOW	*(nods)* I see.
RED:	You won't tell her will you? I didn't mean to and there's no harm done.
YELLOW:	No, I won't tell on you, because I love chocolate too.
SHALIM:	Which only goes to show telling someone a secret means trusting them to keep it.

Do You Believe Me?

Shalim is discovered on. Red enters.

RED:	Have you got any sticky tape, Shalim?
SHALIM:	No. What do you want it for?
RED:	To put across my big fat mouth.
SHALIM:	But why?
RED:	Then I can't talk. That way I won't get into trouble. So go away, Shalim.
SHALIM:	Who has frightened you?
RED:	It's our little secret, that's what he said.
SHALIM:	Who?

RED:	Chas, my sister's boyfriend. I saw him with another girl. He said it was our little secret and it didn't mean anything but if I told my sister, she wouldn't believe me and he'd say it was me that was lying and he'd get me into trouble. But it's true. I saw him with my own eyes. Do you believe me, Shalim?
SHALIM:	Yes. Thank you for telling me. You must have felt very scared.
RED:	What shall I do?
SHALIM:	What do you want to do?
RED:	Leave it. But if he threatens me again, I want to come and tell you so that I can be safe.
SHALIM:	Okay! That's a really good idea. I'll always be here for you.

(Shalim puts his hand out and Red shakes it and then exits.)

SHALIM:	(To the audience) In fact, it didn't take long before Red's sister knew the truth. The girl Chas was seeing behind her back told her herself. She stopped going out with him immediately.

(Red re-enters.)

RED:	And when I told her what Chas had said to me, she was really angry with him and hugged me. She's all right, my sister, and it was all right in the end.
SHALIM:	*(to the audience)* Which only goes to show if someone is hurting you and tells you to keep it secret, it's all right to tell someone you trust.

(Red and Shalim shake hands again and exit.)

Tell You Later

GREEN:	I…I want to tell you something.
BLUE:	What is it?
GREEN:	It's…
BLUE:	What?
GREEN:	Well… Well, I've been meaning to tell you for ages. I really want to tell you.
BLUE:	What do you want to tell me?

GREEN:	It's…it's…*(desperately)* Have you heard the joke about the egg?
BLUE:	No, but is that really what you want to tell me?
GREEN:	It goes like this. 'Waiter, waiter, this egg is bad.' And the waiter says: 'Don't blame me, I only laid the table.' Ha, ha. Just like that. It's the way I tell 'em.
BLUE:	Is that really what you wanted to tell me? Wasn't there something else you wanted to tell me?
GREEN:	Yes, but I'm not ready yet. Tell you later!
BLUE:	OK. Whenever.

(Green and Blue go their separate ways. Rani enters.)

RANI:	(To the audience) The next day.

(Green and Blue enter.)

BLUE:	Hi Green, how are you doing?
GREEN:	Hi. I think I'm ready to tell now.
BLUE:	What is it?
GREEN:	Last term your coat was torn and no one knows how it happened. You left it in the changing room. Do you remember?
BLUE:	Yes, of course, I do.
GREEN:	It was me. I tripped over my back, put my hand out to break my fall and your coat pocket just fell off, kind of thing, all by itself.
BLUE:	You did it?
GREEN:	It was an accident.
BLUE:	Why didn't you tell me?
GREEN:	I thought you'd be cross.
BLUE:	But it was an accident.
GREEN:	Yes, it was. I'm sorry. I was frightened to say.
BLUE:	That's okay but next time, tell me. Then I can tell my Mum what happened.
GREEN:	*(nodding)* Okay. Sorry.

RANI: Which goes to show you can wait until you are ready to tell someone something you've been keeping secret.

It's a Secret!

RED: Hi, Yellow. Do you know what day it is today?

YELLOW: What?

RED: Today is… but hold on a second. You've got to promise… Can you keep a secret?

YELLOW: It depends what it is.

RED: It's a good one, more of a surprise really. And you only have to keep your mouth shut for about six minutes.

YELLOW: Tell me then.

RED: Today is Blue's birthday.

YELLOW: So.

RED: We're planning a surprise. Can you help us?

YELLOW: How?

RED: You're a good singer. Teach us all to sing Happy Birthday when Blue comes.

YELLOW: When is Blue coming?

RED: In about five minutes.

YELLOW: That sounds great. But why didn't you tell me before? I could've…

                 (Blue enters.)

                 Oh hello Blue. Happy…Happy…

                 (Red and Yellow look at Yellow.)

                 Hap…Have a banana.

BLUE: Oh, hello. I'll be back. Just going to see if the post has arrived.

                 (Blue leaves.)

RED: And you ask me why we didn't tell you before! You almost spoiled it – and let the secret out!

YELLOW:	Doesn't Blue look depressed? As if everybody has forgotten his birthday. I bet he's gone to see if the postman has brought any cards.
RED:	But we haven't forgotten, have we? Let's all sing Happy Birthday when Blue comes back. Do you all know it? Quick, before Blue comes back.
YELLOW:	Sure.
	(The puppets teach everyone the song. As they finish, Blue re-enters shyly.)
RED:	Here's Blue.
YELLOW:	Hi, Blue. We've got a surprise for you.
RED:	We have. One, two, three.
	(Yellow leads the song with all puppets and participants joining in. Blue is bashful and delighted.)
BLUE:	Oh thank you everyone… thank you. That was such a lovely surprise. I thought everyone had forgotten it was my birthday.
SHALIM:	Which goes to show secrets which are meant to give someone a surprise – like a birthday party – are positive and good.

5.11   A Puppet Play of Your Own   10 minutes

Have the participants' puppets ready for them on trays but out of sight until this moment of the workshop. Before bringing the puppets out, ask the group to remember back to Body, the workshop in which they made their own puppets. Next, hold up the map of the workshop journey. The participants now get into pairs to make up a puppet play of their own about any of the themes explored so far: trust, power, body, feelings and communicating. They can re-tell a story or act out one of the plays they have seen, or, better still, make up a totally new and unique play of their own. The plays are to be no longer than two minutes at the most, and will be performed as part of Learning. Now it's time to rehearse. After the participants have paired up, give out the puppets. Be on hand to help, stimulate and encourage ideas. Try and get plays on all five workshop themes. Stress the plays must be short, and, if you feel confident of supporting a multilingual approach, allow them to be in any language. Warn the participants when only three minutes of rehearsal time are left and urge them to remember their work for the performance proper in the next session. When their rehearsal is over, ask the group to put their puppets carefully and safely back on the trays and let them know you are looking forward to seeing their plays.

Closing   5 minutes

5.12   Tipping the Wink

Finally, the group move back into the centre of the space for this standing circle observation game which has a sharp focus on the tiniest of communication gestures: the wink. Select someone across the circle, look straight at them, and wink. They, in turn, acknowledge receipt of the wink by winking back. Then they select someone else in the circle and tip the wink to them. Everyone else, when not winked at or winking, tries to follow the winks around the circle; which is not at all easy. With groups who might have difficulty with concentration, it is possible to start the game with the more exaggerated nod-and-a-wink. The challenge of eye contact is further developed now in this closing exercise which makes for a precise and calm ending as this exercise depends on being able to look directly at someone eye-to-eye, so that they know they are the intended recipient, even before the wink is tipped. A successful passing of the wink can give the reassurance that messages, even small ones, can and do get through. And as with most of the exercises, achievement of the modest task can help participants who have internalised a fear of risking failure to feel more confident. The game also practises being receptive to small messages and being aware of others and their attempts to communicate with you. Before ending the group, remind them that the next workshop is about learning and that it is the last one of all and tell them its starting time and venue.

CHAPTER 8

Workshop Six: Learning

This last workshop, *Learning*, approaches its theme in two ways. It presents a review of the five preceding sessions, repeating the learning process in miniature. It simultaneously poses questions about the process or journey itself, inviting the participants to be lucid, conscious and articulate about what they have learnt and how – an ambitious objective and one which may not be ful-filled immediately. Put metaphorically, working with younger participants especially is like buying clothes for them: sometimes you buy clothes a size or two too big so that the wearer may grow into them. A thought, idea, or connection may lie dormant for a long time before it is needed or understood by the participant. This is one of the most optimistic aspects of these workshops – that they can imply a creative future and offer alternatives for those coming times.

Learning directly connects with self-esteem. Authentic learning which happens as a result of interest and trust raises self-esteem, and that change can cause real intelligence in taking care of oneself practically and experientially. Practice in taking learning risks and in improving relationship skills with others can lessen fear of failure and boost confidence so that when mistakes are inevitably made or things don't work out, they can be tolerated by the perfectionists amongst the participants – who are often the participants who give the most contrary impression and seem to be unruly and agitated.

The importance of memory in relation to learning has several aspects. As well as being what the learning processes adheres to, it provides a touchstone for making new decisions and taking what could otherwise appear to be unappealing risks. In abusive situations, memory and memories can be held hostage by feelings and buried in the body in habitual tensions and some kinds of illness. The actuality of experience might be intolerably painful, to such a degree that it is too much to be borne consciously, particularly by younger participants. Then memory is suspended as a means to survival. Amongst those that cause pain and reduce the power and self-esteem of others memory can also be selective: 'it wasn't me', 'I didn't know' resulting in a culpable naiveté. In this session, memory is stimulated in relation to learning which thus enables the play of imagination.

Another crucial underlying issue in this last workshop is how to part, and cope with all the feelings of parting without this having a deleterious effect on the value of the work shared and the memory of it. Even though something is coming to an end for both the participants and for you, it is important to recall it, thus incorporating what was important to us inside ourselves.

For *Learning*, collect all the resources that have been created in the workshop journey, the brainstorm sheets, the puppets and drawings, and display them in the workshop space. Sometimes, we are so sure we won't forget something and then we are amazed when, having cheerfully forgotten all about it, it is brought back to memory again. You may be surprised at the amount of work you and the participants have done, and also at how long ago the first workshop seems.

The workshop opens with familiar methods and exercises. What is different is that it anticipates a series of developments in which the participants are given more opportunities to be effective and to apply their knowledge in learning situations. The warm up reprises exercises and games already known but within quite a long sequence which the participants are asked to remember.

This activity of remembering is continued in the next section of the workshop which goes back on the preceding five taking one exercise from each and either repeating it or extending it. This sequence of five exercises ends with a brainstorm and a report-back from the three groups on what has been learnt, what especially remembered, and what was of particular importance for them. The main effect of this particular report-back is to reinforce the shared language the participants now possess through doing the workshops, that 'language' being a composite one which includes and validates individual languages, sign or other gestural languages and mime, and all the other extended ways of communicating that you have explored. This shared language is the means by which the participants can talk about things that they may not have had names for before – feelings, types of behaviour, needs, rights, voices, stories. This language is now shared between you and will continue to be available even when the workshops have finished.

Next come the participants' plays and their preparation. The main purpose of the performance of these plays is to underline the two-way process of communication: they have listened to the stories and plays prepared for them and now, using their own puppets which they have made and named, they perform for the rest of the group and for you, knowing that you will be listening to them and listening to them not just in the sense of being open to what they are saying, but in a formal, we-are-the-audience way. You may also be documenting or recording these plays. This is a logical extension of all the other ways you have listened to the participants from the beginning: as interested facilitators, as scribes in brainstorm groups, as listeners in the report-back sessions, as well as recorders on tape and video. Becoming an audience for the participants is a formal statement of your willingness to listen to whatever they have to say on whatever theme from the workshops they have chosen.

The last puppet play, *The Parting Poem*, is about an ending in the past and it involves all the puppets, both the colours and the elephant and dragon, in a leave-taking. From the sequence of *Shabbash* stories and plays, it is verbally the most sophisticated of all the plays or stories, using language which is closest to the way that younger participants speak and express themselves. This is designed to focus on the colour puppets particularly as images of positive identity figures. The play also asks its audience to participate by repeating and perhaps learning a short piece about parting.

For the closing exercise of the last workshop comes an exercise based on the miming of a knot being tied. It is a symbolic action planted here in the hope that it can bear fruit in two ways. The knot each of the participants mime functions as the making of a memory. In metaphorical terms: you make a knot in order to remember something; you mark a particular painful or joyful event in your life; you keep a tight hold on something that is important for you: a feeling, a moment, a discovery; you keep it for the future, for a time when you will be ready to remember it and perhaps tell someone. Second, it marks the relatedness of the individuals and the group, however anarchic or frail some of those relationships still seem. This knot can also be seen as a remembering of a memory. It creates a future or the possibility of one. In metaphorical terms you can go back to a knot you tied, which may now be quite a tight one; you could begin to unravel the interwoven strands and as you do so, you can remember the circumstances, feelings and meanings of the knot. You might now remember why it was that you tied the knot in the first place. You might then find that now is the moment, no longer in the future, for which you made the knot. You might even find that you now no longer need to keep remembering that particular knot on your own, but want to tell somebody about it.

The workshop ends with goodbyes and in the knowledge that learning never ends and how much of what we learn about the world and ourselves happens through the agency of relationship. Be sure before beginning this workshop that you have prepared yourself for the end of the journey so that you can lead the participants creatively, consciously and safely right through to the finish.

Workshop Six – Learning

Contents

Introduction to the sixth workshop

Warm up exercises

Materials

- name tags
- the map of the workshop sessions
- large sheets of paper and markers
- pencils and papers
- the participants' puppets with their rulers
- the colour puppets and elephant and dragon puppets
- a puppet stage (optional)
- a camera (optional)
- transition objects (optional): small photocopied maps of the journey, a folder of the stories and plays of the workshops, the words of the Parting Poem.

Introduction to the sixth workshop   5 minutes

Begin the workshop in the usual way, seated on the floor, in a circle. Hold up the map of the journey from which it will be clear that this sixth session, *Learning*, is the last of these workshops you and the participants will share together. Name the workshop in as many languages as you can from within the group. Recall the names of the other sessions and point out how much you have been through together, and how much you have experienced. Ask the group if they think they have learned from the workshops. If so, how did they learn? Let this be an informal enquiry, not a brainstorm, not written down. Some of the responses might be: 'from you', 'from each other', 'from the puppets', 'by doing', 'by talking', 'by acting', 'by laughing', or best of all, 'because we wanted to.' This is the last workshop, and there may be some sad feelings. Because a whole workshop still lies ahead, it is best to keep this introduction light, precise, and brief. End by saying that having thought about how we learn it is time to look at and remember some of what has been learnt.

Warm up exercises   5 minutes

6.1   The Warm Up Sequence

By now, through increased confidence and familiarity, the group should be able to remember and sustain a sequence of warm up exercises. Tell the group the sequence and ask them to remember it. Before they can forget or think that they will, get everyone up on their feet and begin. The warm up sequence should be done without a break and, if possible, without specific comment from yourself to any individual in the group or to the group as a whole. You will find that doing several exercises one after the other in this way will produce a strong energy with the participants coming together dynamically. This is an energy which you can take into the main body of the workshop. The warm up sequence is as follows:

- the *Relax Button* done three times
- *Shaking All Over*
- *Shake And Freeze 2*
- *Warm Up Faces*
- and finally, *Breathing 5*.

Finish the sequence by giving the group another count of three to take a sixth breath. Release this by letting the breath out in a clear, strong, sung 'ah' sound which you can hold for as long as you think good, but don't sustain the note too long if the effort is causing tensions in the upper chests. Give the participants positive feedback not only for remembering the sequence but also for trying and learning something new, that is, the singing out of the sixth breath.

Recalling the journey   20 minutes

6.2   Palm to Person

In this part of the workshop, the group reprise and, in some cases, vary or extend a series of exercises recalling each stage of the workshop process. The first exercise is a development of *Palm To Palm* from *Trust*, the first workshop. In the context of this last workshop the exercise becomes not only about trust but also a measure of any increase in trust that the group might have gained from doing this work. The experience of being able to trust more and to see that reflected in this practical way is to give physical embodiment to a quality which has been learned. Demonstrate this exercise with another facilitator if you are part of a team, or if facilitating these sessions alone, ask the two participants most similar to you in height and weight to join you. Ask one, A, to stand between you and the other participant, B, facing you. Slightly bend the knees so that the weight is over both feet in a position of strength and balance. Both you and participant B raise your palms until they are poised either side of A's shoulders. When A feels ready, invite him or her, keeping their eyes open all the while, to rest their weight forward against your hands. Support A, taking his or her weight into your body, then gently return him or her to the vertical. Then ask A to lean back onto B's hands. Be very watchful at this time and be clear with B that they are ready themselves to take A's weight and support it. Then get A to rock forwards to you, and then back to B. Once A feels secure rocking to and fro, and if you feel confident of their being able to take the challenge, ask them to close their eyes. This is quite a demand on A's level of trusting. If you have any doubts, it is better to stay within what the participants can manage rather than risk a loss of balance through being too ambitious on their behalf. Never give A any cause for anxiety, and do not let him or her lean any further than she did first – though this could be a development of the exercise for participants who are either older or physically skilful. Throughout the demonstration make reassuring remarks and enquire how A is feeling. Finish demonstrating by holding A's shoulders and bringing them to stillness and letting them know they can open their eyes. After the demonstration, ask the group to say what they think helped A to trust both yourself and B and then check these answers out with A. This demonstration may take some minutes, but don't be tempted to hurry. The success of trust work is often in the setting up. Divide the group into threes, and get everyone ready to do the exercise. Explain that each person will have a turn in the middle and two turns as a supporter. As the threes get to work, circulate, helping and advising where necessary, while everyone tries it. It is probably almost certain that you will notice a marked physical improvement in balance and relatedness. The workshops do make participants more trusting. Not everyone will be perfect, but you may notice that even those children who have had previous difficulties in trusting and accepting trust, will show signs of improvement. One or two participants may be eager to play the obvious trick of letting the one in the middle fall too far, expressing so graphically perhaps how when they themselves had expected someone to be there, they weren't.

6.3   Greetings from on High

To recall *Power,* next comes a status game which has not been done before but which offers both a chance to remember the theme, and a chance to celebrate something learned. The object of this game is to provide a brief acting context in which to express self-confidence and feeling powerful in body and voice. Ask the group to sit on the floor in a circle whilst setting a chair in the circle for yourself. Explain that each participant is to greet you by saying 'good morning' or 'hello' in any language they choose. The aim of the game is for each person to greet you in a way that makes them feel powerful and you 'incy', to refer back to *Incy and Falloon*s of the same *Power* workshops; or, to use a more technical term, to give themselves higher status than you. Go round the circle with each participant standing up to greet you one by one. Don't be tempted to let the participants greet you in a random order. That may leave room for the more timid participants to miss out their turn. Allow any language as many of the group will communicate their increased feeling of power by using their own language just as some will raise their voice or increase their height. This game, an anarchic and radical reversal of the power dynamics between facilitator and participants, is fun, and lets everyone show an increased confidence if they want to. It is also a reminder that being powerful is not necessarily hurtful but can be enjoyable and enabling, showing that powerfulness is not necessarily fixed by your size and physical strength.

6.4   Frozen Statues

Body is next. Looking at the brainstorm sheets you have displayed on the walls, remind the group of the brainstorms they did on 'Things that make your body feel good – things that you like doing'. You will find in most cases the group will not need to refer to the sheets because they can remember their ideas. Ask them each to choose one activity from that brainstorm. It can be their own suggestion or one of someone else's. The group think about it and then and make it into a 'frozen' statue of that activity. Give the participants a minute to prepare, then everyone returns to the circle and going round the circle, one by one, shows their frozen statue. Again the objective is to build on memory and extend and develop its possibilities, in other words, to try to create space for an optimism which in its turn may be more inclined to suggest a creative future rather than an inevitable apocalypse. Here the remembered theme of *Body* is summed up with a precise positive physical image chosen by the participant himself or herself.

6.5   All Our Feelings

For *Feelings* sit the group down in the circle again. Get a marker pen and a large sheet of paper. The group try to remember all the different feelings and different words for different feelings they have learned while you write them down. This is not a brainstorm, there is no strict time limit, rather it is something you all do together, not to elicit information and chronicle it, but to share. Remind the group of any omissions (they may be polite enough to leave out 'boring' or 'confusion') and also add other feelings in, if appropriate. The significance of this remembering about feelings lies in the process everyone on the workshops has been through. The group have moved through the physical shapes of their animal transformations to expressing feelings in and through the body, then to feelings expressed in the face, and through the use of other languages and the emotionality of mimed or otherwise acted-out feelings. During the workshops, the group have been enabled to go from one feeling to another within the safe framework of exercises combining feelings, power and trust. The crucial learning here is about choice: that you feel something, but you can choose what you do – you don't have to act on it or act it out. Point out that while everyone has been learning, they have also been opening up to learning a whole new vocabulary of feeling, one shared with the facilitators, and that after the workshops are over, that talking about feelings will still remain a possible and valid thing to do.

6.6   Brainstorm 5

For *Communicating*, the fifth and most recent workshop, the activity by which it is recalled is not so much a memory of the workshop from two days before, as a summing up and writing down of all the themes from all the sessions. In their three groups for the last time, the participants now have the chance to communicate to you and each other everything they like, have been interested in and have learned from all of the workshops. Give each group a large sheet of paper and the following instructions: 'You have five minutes to record:

- things that you have learned
- things that you especially remembered

- things that were particularly important for you.'

In most cases, you and the other facilitators will probably write the suggestions down but in a group where the participants are quick and happy with writing, let them write for themselves. Their sheets will surely include lists, incidents from the plays, messages from the stories, evaluations of the games, and many thoughtful words of advice on self-protection and the rights of the participants from the participants themselves. After their five minutes, the three groups now return to the Listening Corner to report back.

Relating and creating   30 minutes

6.7   A Puppet Play of Your Own 2

The group now arrive at doing something difficult which deliberately involves both memory and imagining an activity in the future. In the last workshop *Communication*, the group began to plan their own puppet play on one of the workshop themes to be performed in this last workshop, *Learning*. Then, they were given the puppets they made in *Body* and, in pairs, a short time to talk and think about what they would do. Remind them of this, dealing with the buzz of excitement and anxiety as you do so. Tell the group that they have ten minutes now to devise and rehearse. As this is not much time, it is better that the plays be short so that everyone's can be seen. Explain that in the ten minutes they have to make the plays up, they will be working in their same pairs and that after the plays are over, the puppets are theirs to keep. Give out the puppets and let the participants pair up and get to work. Inevitably, a few participants will be without partners or their original partner will be absent. Sort out new arrangements as speedily as you can.

Performing a play is a symbolic and not always an easy step. Some of the participants may not choose to take it. If so, and if you feel this is an appropriate alternative, these participants can write letters to the puppet they like best instead, or to the puppet whose story has impressed them most. Have pencils and papers standing by for this.

Be strict with the timing, letting the participants know when they have had half their preparation time. At the end of the rehearsal period, everyone goes back to the Listening Corner which may have some simple stage or performing area in front of it. Ask for the first play. Some pairs may prepare a play but in the event will not want to perform it. If you feel this reticence is more than simple shyness which they can be coaxed through, let them have the choice to perform or not. After seeing some of their peers' plays, they may change their mind. If some of the plays ramble, intervene so that everyone has time for their work to be seen. Make no judgement or criticism on the content or presentation as the plays perform. See and accept them. If some of the plays are in different languages, a participant who can speak the languages involved can interpret the play for the audience while the actors perform, or the actors themselves can say something about the play before they perform it in the language or languages of their choice. You may well find that students who have English as a second language use more English in their puppet plays than they generally speak in a whole school day.

Record the plays and any letters to the puppets on tape and, if possible, take a photograph of each play. You may be surprised by the content of the plays. Some of them may be inventive; some retellings of stories already told. These retellings are both valuable in themselves and as clues to the way different participants have made the stories their own. You might want to transcribe the plays at a later date or have them documented in some form for others, not involved in the journey, to see and enjoy.

6.8   Puppet Play 14: The Parting Poem   5 minutes

Fittingly, this last puppet play, involving all the puppets, is about endings and saying goodbyes. One of the tasks of this last session is convey the possibility that relationships can endure in spite of change and separation with their significance altered, not destroyed by a physical parting. How to end relation-ships is one of the hardest choices any of us have to make. Here a model is given which is designed not only to provide the narrative content of the last puppet play in the workshop journey but also as a paradigm of how you and the participants can part from the workshop process while still continuing to value it when it ends. If you are facilitating with others, share the puppets between you. If not, lie all the puppets out, including the elephant and the dragon puppet, on a table in front of you, or similarly convenient surface, to enable you to make the simplest, easiest moves. It may be that you do not even put your hand inside the puppets to animate them but hold them like dolls for greater simplicity in acting out the final puppet play. This play is from the *Shabbash* sequence of plays and is repeated in story order in that section.

The Parting Poem

DRAGON: This is a story about saying goodbye.

RANI: Saying goodbye can be the hardest thing in the world, but we all have to sometimes. Red, Green and Blue…

            (Presents puppets.)

DRAGON:	All went to the same nursery school when they were very small.

(The Dragon turns to the colour puppets.)

Do you remember?

BLUE:	Oh yes! That's where I met the first person who I ever remember being kind and loving – Yellow.

(Presents Yellow.)

RANI:	*(to the audiences)* Yellow was their nursery school teacher.
RED:	She was beautiful.
BLUE:	She always had a warm smile.
RED:	With which she welcomed us in the mornings.
GREEN:	She used to give hugs that were really comforting.
BLUE:	My thoughts about her are always dreamy.
RED:	I always picture her on a sunny day.

(Yellow leaves.)

BLUE:	Red and Green and I left the nursery when we were old enough to go to Big School, as we called it.
GREEN:	We meant primary school.
BLUE:	We felt very sad saying goodbye to Yellow.
RANI:	And it was sunny on that day.
RED:	Which day?
DRAGON:	The Colours' last day at nursery.
RED:	Our last day at nursery.

(Yellow enters.)

YELLOW:	Good morning. Asalaam wai alaicum. Bon jour.
GREEN & BLUE:	*(sadly, to Yellow)* Wai alaicum salaam.
RED:	Bon jour, Miss. Good morning.
GREEN:	We're going to miss you a lot.
YELLOW:	I'll miss you too. But whenever you do, remember this 'Whatever is in front of us –'
BLUE:	'Whatever is in front of us…'

YELLOW:	'Whatever is behind us…'
RED:	'Whatever is behind us…'
YELLOW:	'Is nothing compared to…'
GREEN:	'Is nothing compared to…'
YELLOW:	'What is between us.'
GREEN, RED & BLUE:	'What is between us.'
YELLOW:	Can you remember that?
RED:	Yes.
YELLOW:	That's brilliant. You are clever.
BLUE & GREEN:	Bye.

(They hug her quickly and walk away. Yellow exits.)

RED:	Bye! Bye!

(He hugs her and runs off, stopping for one last wave. Yellow exits.)

BLUE:	Gone. Why am I so upset?
GREEN:	You're just missing her.
BLUE:	Don't tell anyone else.
RED:	Huh?
GREEN:	Don't tell anyone else.
RED:	Right.
BLUE:	Right. I hope we never have to part.
GREEN:	We've always been friends. We always will be.
RED:	Whatever is in front of us…
GREEN:	Whatever is behind us is nothing…
RED, BLUE & GREEN:	Compared to what is between us.
RANI:	And although they grew up and many things happened to them, they never did forget her.

(Yellow enters again.)

DRAGON:	And she never forgot them.

RANI:	*(to the audience)* And we will never forget you.
DRAGON:	(To the audience) Can we say the parting poem together?
	(Allows the audience to answer.)
RANI:	'Whatever is in front of us...'
EVERYONE:	'Whatever is in front of us...'
RANI:	'Whatever is behind us...'
EVERYONE:	'Whatever is behind us...'
DRAGON:	'Is nothing compared to...'
EVERYONE:	'Is nothing compared to...'
DRAGON:	'What is between us.'
EVERYONE:	'What is between us.'
RANI:	Brilliant! You are clever!
DRAGON:	Thank you!
RED, BLUE, & GREEN:	Bye! Bye! Goodbye!
	(The Colour Puppets exit in the puppet bag, followed by Rani and the Dragon. The puppet bag is shut.)

Closing   10 minutes

6.9   The Knot

Allow as little time after the puppet play has finished as you can before moving on to these closing exercises. This brief exercise is the key for the ending of the workshop journey and its last remaining minutes. The participants leave the Listening Corner and come and join you in a standing circle. Say that you are going to mime tying a knot in a piece of string and do so. Pick up an imaginary piece of string and make a knot in it. Ask the group to do the same. Explain that tying a knot in a piece of string is a way of remembering something. Now say that each one of you, including yourself, is to think of one thing they want to remember from this journey and to think of it when they tie their imaginary knot so they don't forget it. Repeat the mime bearing in mind the thing remembered, which is private and does not have to be spoken aloud or shared in any way although some participants might want to tell you. If so, let them. Accept that and listen without comment, but acknowledge their contribution.

6.10   Goodbyes

If you are not going to see the group again, say your goodbyes. If you are continuing to work together, then this is the time to mark the end of this particular stage in your work. It may be that you want to mark this ending by giving gifts, transition objects, much like going-away presents at a party – to keep and hold close when something finishes or someone you have become attached to goes away. Perhaps you might like to give a folder containing all the stories and plays that have been part of the workshops or photocopies of the map of the journey with the words of the *Parting Poem*, or to take another photograph, this time of the whole group together or find another way to mark your communal achievement and create an appropriate and affirming ending. It is up to you. Next, if you feel this is appropriate, start the *Parting Poem* and say it together. Finally, thank the participants for coming on this journey with you as this is now the end of the last workshop, *Learning*, which itself never ends. In order to end the journey and to celebrate all your work together give the participants and yourself applause. Everyone will join in. And then end.

CHAPTER 9

More True Stories

These true stories, all of which have been used as part of the *Trust And Power* workshops, form an additional resource providing choice and alternatives as part of the main body of workshop text. They can be used in different workshops, according to the age and the needs of those involved. However, while they appear in alphabetical order, the workshop they originally illustrated and supported is identified here with suggestions as to other workshops which they could go with. With the exception of one story which has two parts, they are presented without questions for discussion in order to provide more flexibility. If the story is to be used for discussion purposes, the clearest approach is to ask questions about the story itself, the dilemmas of the characters, how the various characters were feeling and ideas for what happened after the story ended, and if anything could have been done to resolve or ameliorate the situation or dilemma of the protagonists.

Claudia's Uncle

Definitely for participants over the age of twelve, this story is appropriate for *Feelings* but could equally well be a story for *Body, Trust,* or *Power.*

NARRATOR: This is a true story. When Claudia was about ten years old,...

(Presents green puppet.)

...she went on holiday to Turkey with her family and her mother's sister's husband's family. She got these feelings about her uncle which didn't feel right.

(Presents blue puppet.)

One day, they went to the beach and they were playing in the water, running and splashing and jumping. Her uncle joined them and jumped about and jumped on Claudia for fun like everyone else was, but it didn't feel right.

(The puppets act this out. The uncle leaves Claudia who is thoughtful and alone.)

When she was fourteen, she still felt these very strange feelings about him which did not feel right but she didn't understand.

(Claudia moves and the mood changes.)

When she was sixteen, she went to Israel. She was very excited about going.

(Claudia and the uncle meet each other.)

Her uncle met her at the airport and they went back to his mother's place to sleep. There was a double bed in the room and a single. He said, 'Sleep in the double.'

Claudia lay down, and her uncle lay next to her. She didn't know quite what was wrong, but it was very strange. Next he said, 'Are you sleeping?'

She didn't reply. She was shaking like a leaf. Then he put his arm round her. She asked him, 'What are you doing?'

'Nothing. Do you want to have sex with me?'

Claudia was shocked. She said, 'You must be mad.'

She turned her back on him, and started to cry. They lay there until about seven o'clock. She felt angry, sad, confused, a whole range of emotions. Then she thought 'I'm going to ask him why he did that.' And she did. He told her that she looked very like his wife, Helen, who was seven months pregnant, so he couldn't have sex with her. Claudia said to him, 'I can't believe you did that.'

Then the others arrived. He drove everyone up north. And before he left, he said, 'You're not going to tell your mother.'

'I can't promise that,' Claudia replied.

(The uncle leaves.)

Claudia went home and told her mother everything, but they decided to keep it all between the two of them. Claudia still sees her uncle. Everyone thinks the world of him, but Claudia never lets him touch her when he greets her. When Claudia told me this story, she said,

'I'd like other people to hear my story so that anyone else who may have been in a similar situation knows that they are not alone, and that they don't have to feel guilty.'

Coral's Dog, Judy

This story can be an alternative story in *Feelings*. If so, it should come after *Mina's Kitten*, with the opening lines providing the link. It could also be used in *Trust*, as an example of trust being broken, or in *Power* with the participants being asked to consider the power of each of the people in the story, including perhaps the dog herself.

NARRATOR: This story is a little bit like Mina's about her kitten, and it really happened to a girl called Coral, who was about eleven. The point is that telling somebody how you feel can help. It can change the feelings and make you feel better, but this a story about what happened to Coral when she had lots of feelings going on inside her, and it wasn't possible for her to talk about them.

(The Narrator presents the puppet.)

Coral was about eleven. At that time, she didn't live in a city but in a very cold house right in the middle of a wood. In the woods were some wild pigs and they used to cry in the middle of the night with a really scary noise. To be honest with you, at this time in her life Coral was lonely. None of her friends lived near her. It was a long walk to the nearest house, but she had one friend, her dog Judy. Judy was black and white. She was a mongrel, she was a bit of sheepdog, a bit of spaniel, a bit of this and that. She had the most beautiful brown eyes, and Coral loved her. They played together.

(Coral stands up straight.)

Now, the time came when it was the summer and Coral and her mother and father went away on holiday. They couldn't take Judy with them so they left Judy with Coral's friends at the end of the long road, at the other end of the road. They were called the Hills. Mrs. Hill and Jenny Hill. And they were looking after Judy while Coral and her Mum and Dad were away.

(Coral waves to her dog and goes away.)

When Coral came back from holiday, the first thing she
wanted to do was to see Judy.

(Coral re-enters with another of the colour puppets as her mother.)
She said, 'Mum, Mum, I'm going to go up to the Hills and
get Judy.'

Her mother said, 'Oh, all right.'

So she walked up the long road and she arrived at the Hills'
house. She knocked on the door and Jenny Hill came out.

(The Narrator represents another of the colour puppets as Jenny.)

'Hello,' she said. 'Did you have a nice holiday?'

'Yes,' said Coral, 'I've come to collect Judy, where is she?'

Jenny said, 'Oh, didn't you know? Your Mum asked us to
take her to the vet to have her put to sleep, to have her put
down.'

Coral had no idea that this was going to happen. And she
just said, 'Oh, right, I forgot.' Being 'put to sleep' or 'being
put down' means that the dog was dead.

(Jenny goes off and Coral walks slowly and sadly back to her home.)

Coral walked back home. And she never said anything about
it. And she never cried, even though she loved Judy so
much.

And it wasn't until about fifteen years later, when she was
talking to some friends about dogs, that she suddenly
remembered Judy and she just started crying. But she never
cried at the time, and she'd never told anyone how she felt.

Joey's Call to ChildLine

This again is a story only for use with participants older than twelve. It is for
Communication and will need some careful discussion along with questions
that are sensitive and empathetic.

NARRATOR: This is a story about a young girl who had to grow up very
quickly and who was very unhappy. This is Joey, and this is a
story about what happened to her.

(Presents red puppet.)

JOEY: *(to the audience)* This is what happened to me. I was nearly eleven when the sexual abuse started. I had no one to talk to, no friends that I could trust. I couldn't tell my parents as it was another member of the family who was abusing me. I needed and wanted to talk to someone. I spent hours alone with my dog just crying into his fur. He was comforting but he could not talk to me. I decided one day when I felt strong to ring ChildLine. Everyone at school was saying how good it was and helpful, so I went for a walk.

(Joey acts this out.)

I went to the 'phone box about a mile away from home, a 'phone box with very little happening around it. I called Directory Enquires. The operator got me the number, one which repeated over and over so it could be remembered. Still feeling brave, I picked up the phone and dialled. It rang. I panicked and put down the phone. I could not do it. I fled the 'phone box in tears.

(Joey runs off.)

The next day, I went again to the same 'phone box.

(Joey comes back on again.)

Picking up the 'phone, dialling the number, I was scared, so scared. I thought they would know who I was, where I was, what I looked like. The tears would not stop falling. The line was engaged. I didn't move, just listened to the engaged tone, and finally put down the phone. I tried again. It rang and someone said 'Hello'. It was too much. I burst into tears. I could not say anything. The voice kept saying 'Take your time, it's okay. Tell me your name. You don't have to give me your real one.' I was so frightened, I put down the phone and ran.

(Joey runs away and then reappears, looking very low.)

I was so ashamed not only of what was happening to me but also of not having the strength to talk to someone, someone who was there especially to help and listen to me.

(Joey moves to the 'phone box again.)

A few days later I went again to the 'phone box and dialled the ChildLine number. I got through. I fought back the tears

for all of ten seconds then just let go. The person on the
other end just listened to me, told me to go on, just listened
like nobody has ever done for me, even though as it came
out it probably didn't make much sense. It came out so fast,
in bursts, intermingled with tears and gasps for air. It made
me feel much better, equipped to handle what was
happening, and realising that it was not me who was in the
wrong.

Marcia and Tamsin

Here is another story about someone misusing their power with a slightly
different format which can be used instead of *Ralph and Jane* or in addition to
that story in *Power*. If the emphasis is on the dilemmas of the characters, then
this story can be part of *Feelings*. The story is told in two parts. After the first, the
group discuss and respond to the dilemmas of the two protagonists, and
rehearse and act out their solutions to the situation. After they have done this,
the story continues with the actual outcome of this true story.

NARRATOR: This is a true story.

(Presents red puppet.)

Marcia was eleven years old. She had just started a new
school, in the middle of the term, and had only been there a
few weeks. One day Tamsin,

(Presents blue puppet.)

who was very shy and quiet, was sitting alone in the
classroom writing; she was waiting for the class to begin.
Marcia walked into the classroom and saw Tamsin.

(The puppets act this out.)

'Oh…look. It's goody-goody Tamsin,' she said. Tamsin
looked up and saw Marcia.

(The puppets act this out.)

She closed her book, and tried to hide it. But Marcia crept
up behind Tamsin, and snatched the book away. 'Oh…I see
goody-goody's done all her homework. And I bet she'll get
them all right as well. Well I think they are all wrong.' And
with that Marcia threw Tamsin's book to the back of the
classroom. And walked away.

(Marcia exits and rests on the chest of the Narrator.)

Tamsin said nothing. She just sat there and held her head down.'

- How would you describe Marcia's behaviour?
- How is Tamsin feeling?
- If you think she is feeling powerless, what could help her?
- What could she do next?
- What could someone else do?
- Discuss different ways of ending this play. Act them out.

Marcia and Tamsin Continued...

(Presents Marcia.)

NARRATOR: Marcia didn't say sorry then, not that day, not that week, not that month. But later on in the term, she saw how horrible she was being to Tamsin...

(Presents Tamsin.)

...and so she tried to make friends.

(The puppets act this out.)

Tamsin didn't want to make friends, because Marcia had upset her too much. But Marcia felt sorry for what she'd done, and never picked on anyone again.

Robbie's First School and Robbie's Second School

For the workshop *Communication*, this story was told first in British Sign Language and appears now in a written literal English translation. If this renders the story inaccessible for certain groups, it can be adapted into formal spoken English. If it is used with participants who sign then one facilitator acts out the story while a second narrates it in either English or British Sign Language or in Sign Supported English. The first story can be used with any age group. However, Robbie's story continues as he describes his second school. It is included here, but again is only appropriate to groups of older participants.

Robbie's First School

NARRATOR: This story is about a boy called Robbie...

(Presents blue puppet.)

…who was born profoundly deaf and whose first language is sign language.

(Robbie speaks directly to the audience.)

ROBBIE: Me start school age four. At four, no speech, no sign; communication: nothing; body language: nothing. Mother and father treat me like puppet. Old times, thirty years ago. Awareness about deaf community, none, deaf culture none. My father put me in school, aged four. Sleeping school. Every weekend home. At home then, cry, cry, scream.

(Robbie cries and is miserable. He doesn't want to go back to school.)

When my father took me back, communication nothing. He didn't tell me why I was there. Housemother took me, told me 'Stop crying', put me in bed or in corner. Communication nothing, nothing. Worse, worse. It was the same for other deaf students. We were friends in a group. They were only people I could communicate with. We supported each other. Twenty in a dormitory. Went to bed half five. All cry because we didn't know what we were doing in bed. Communication nothing. Then, 'shush!'

(Robbie stealthily puts on the light.)

We put light on. Group communicating, trying to understand what was going on. Housemother came in. Angry. Smack, smack all. Next day, bed half four. We felt angry, frustration. Communication nothing. Housemother did not know how we feel. Mother and Father came pick me up I try tell they about what happen at school but problem – no communication with them.

Hard life all my life.

(Robbie cheers up.)

When I was eight, leave to go big school. Feel more better because more communication with them, use sign language.

Robbie's Second School

(The blue puppet representing Robbie talks directly to the audience.)

ROBBIE: When I was eight, I leave my first school to go big school. Feel more better because more communication with them, use sign language. Move to the new school. Happy. New school sign have, communication have, but bullied sexually, age eleven. Headmaster find me with a man. Angry, hit me with his shoe twenty times. Next day at Prayers, about one hundred people there, he told everyone about me. Ashamed. More bullying, fighting, 'poof!' No friends. Lonely. Everyone ignores me. Man came sexually still but now have about ten boys doing the same to them like to me. Housefather bullies two boy, my good friends. Old times, long ago, everyone thought that was okay. I wish I was a pupil now. Because then gay awareness nothing. I thought I was the only one in the world. I am glad to tell my story because I always always wanted to write the story of my life and publish it in a book.

Saturday Morning Shopping

This story, about unwanted touch, is an alternative to the stories presented in *Body*. A clear and strong piece, it needs to have some discussion following it. Because of the implicitly intrusive actions of the man involved, it is especially important to reflect on what happened in the story and to get the participants to re-tell its events.

NARRATOR: This is a true story about a girl call Celestine.

(Presents green puppet.)

One day she was with her mum.

(Presents yellow puppet.)

She was about eight and she was doing some shopping in the Bullring Shopping Centre which is a big indoor market in Birmingham. It was a Saturday morning and it was absolutely packed as it always is. Her mum was stopping off at all the stalls taking her time and Celestine could see this man following them.

(Celestine looks over her shoulder.)

He looked very big probably because Celestine was so small. Eventually her mum stopped off at a stall which wasn't so crowded. Celestine was standing behind her mum.

(The puppets act this out.)

Then this man came up and started pressing himself against her, and Celestine, in turn, obviously was pushed against her mum. And so her mum who was being pushed turned around and said to Celestine, 'Why are you pushing?' She looked at Celestine's face and then she looked at the man. Celestine could see the expression on her mum's face when she saw the man, and her mum went mad, mad, mad.

(Celestine's Mum is outraged.)

She started calling him all kinds of names and hitting him with her handbag which broke, and he ran off. She ran after him all round the market shouting at him 'You leave my daughter alone, you!' and all the stall owners were saying 'That's right, love, you tell him!' Celestine was dying with embarrassment but she was also relieved.

Tom Burridge's Cap

Originally part of *Power*, this story is also appropriate to *Body* and *Feelings*, according to which aspect of the narrative is emphasised.

NARRATOR: Dilip was about eight or nine. He was going to school on the train on his own and a boy in his year – Tom Burridge –

(Presents blue puppet.)

– was there and they were both crossing over the track by the railway bridge. Dilip came up behind Tom Burridge and for a joke, knocked his cap off. He picked it up and put it back on, and they got talking. On that day, Tom was travelling with his father.

(Presents red puppet.)

His father was really angry that Dilip knocked off Tom's cap. He said, 'What do you think you're doing?'

He told Dilip to bend over. Dilip said, 'No.'

Then he put Dilip over his knees and spanked him in the middle of the crowded station. It was so humiliating. Dilip ran off to the other end of the platform.

(Dilip goes, and Tom and his father exit in the opposite direction.)

He never told anyone. He was too embarrassed and humiliated. He never did tell anyone until now when I asked him for a story to tell you. After telling me, he added:

(Dilip enters again and speaks to the audience directly.)

'If I were ever to meet him again, I would remind Mr. Burridge of the incident. Whether he remembers it or not, I would say,

'For twenty years, I've been hoping to bump into you again. I've been hoping I would bump into you in a crowded place, and I've thought about wanting to punch and embarrass you the same way as you embarrassed me all those years ago. But I know better than that.'

Dilip is still very angry about the whole incident, but he is glad he has spoken about it at last. It made him feel better. And that's what he told me to tell you.

CHAPTER 10

More Plays for the Colours

These plays are a development from the *Trust and Power* workshops, combining many actual responses from participants to such stimuli as the brainstorms and discussions with more stories, all based on real experience, which deepen the central speculations on self-esteem and safety. These short plays feature the Colours, who here develop individual character traits and relationships. Red, Blue and Green are contemporaries while Yellow, often their advocate when they need her, is their former nursery nurse.

While the plays are still intended for performance by the puppets, they can also be performed in an exciting development by the facilitating teams, by actors, or, with care and thoughtful rehearsal, by the participants themselves. The choice of how to present them is full of possibilities but at their simplest, they require only the most basic of stages whether performed by puppets or adults. Accessibility is the key.

Given here in monolingual form as well as multilingually, both the Prologue and the Epilogue are designed so that they can introduce and end all the plays, although it may be that the producing team will like to contextualise the plays in a different way. One of the most important and affirming benefits of multilingualism, particularly on stage, is to see everyone speaking different languages, not only English by those for whom English is a second language but, for example, Somali or Russian being spoken by English first language speakers. One of the plays, *Red's Story*, is presented in a fully multilingual form to show how the juxtaposition of languages can be structured, and is in English, Bengali, and British Sign Language. The Bengali is written phonetically with some of it in the Sylheti dialect, widely spoken in some of the Bangladeshi communities in the United Kingdom; the British Sign Language is written down sign for sign, following its own syntax.

Although each play is a discrete entity, together they form the unfolding story of Red, Blue and Green with the caring figure of Yellow not far in the background. The gender of all four characters is again up to each group but here, notionally, Blue and Red are male, Yellow and Green female. Some of the content of the plays is complex, and deals with severe challenges to safety and self-esteem. This is especially true of some of the latter plays, in particular *Blue's Story*, *Red's Story*, and *Green's Story*, but all these short plays reflect real life, and the real dilemmas with which young people have to cope. In this sequence of plays, Yellow does not tell her story. As advocate of the other Colours, it is not appropriate that she should ask for their attention and risk making them and, more pertinently, the audience feel emotionally responsible for her and her experience.

Follow-up discussions and questions are given here which again can be adapted according to specific use. Perhaps some of these discussions, especially those which offer solutions as to how the characters might proceed, may lead to new plays and new developments for the Colours. The only template to keep to is what is true. To fudge the issues and provide sweet stories for cute characters is to entertain. That we should be entertained is to be wished, but is not the prime objective of these plays, whose intention is to imagine and acknowledge the very real suffering and complexities that many young people endure and which survive with them unresolved into adulthood; and to provide a means to an authentic empowerment built on experience, however painful or joyous that experience has been. These plays are not just for younger participants, but for anyone who feels on behalf of themselves or others that it is never too late to discover the selves we would have been, had we not been hurt.

Prologue

This Prologue can introduce any of the Colours' plays. It can also establish a multilingual presentation of the plays. Given here first only in English, the second version of the Prologue offers a simple example of how three languages may be integrated. Inescapably, languages are linked to power and status which varies from society to society. Consider which language is perceived to have the least status in the group for whom the plays are presented, and choose that language for the first words spoken. English is a language with very high status, and may be placed second or third according to the specifics of the situation. In this example, assuming that it is the most spoken language in this hypothetical group, it takes third place, as Language C.

(Green appears.)

GREEN: We're going to do a play for you.

             (Red appears.)

RED: It's true. We're going to perform a play for you.

             (Blue appears.)

BLUE:	We are going to perform this play for you –
GREEN:	And I play Green.
RED:	I am Red.
BLUE:	And I'll be Blue.
	(Yellow appears.)
YELLOW:	I'm…
	(She looks down at her yellow dress.)
	…Yellow.
BLUE:	The play is called –
ALL:	*(saying the title of the play to follow)…*

Prologue – In Three Languages

BLUE, GREEN & RED:	*(Language A, a language other than English)* We're going to perform a play for you. It's all true.
GREEN:	*(Language B)* We're going to do a play for you. It's all true.
BLUE & RED:	*(Language C)* We're going to perform a play for you. It's all true.
GREEN:	*(A)* We are going to perform this play for you –
RED:	*(C)* In three languages.
BLUE:	*(B)* In English;
GREEN:	*(A)* In [Language A];
RED:	*(B)* And in [Language B].
GREEN:	*(B)* I play Green.
RED:	*(A)* I'm Red….
BLUE:	*(A)* And I'll be Blue.
YELLOW:	*(C)* I'm…
	(She looks down at her yellow dress.)
	…Yellow.
BLUE:	*(A)* The play is called –
ALL:	*(A, saying the title of the play to follow)…*

RED:	*(B, saying the title of the play to follow)*...
GREEN & BLUE:	*(C, saying the title of the play to follow)*...

It All Started the Day We Were Born

In this play, the three Colours, Red, Blue and Green 'remember' being born. Actually, they are reflecting a profound impression of themselves and their identity. Red is disappointed because he was the wrong gender, Blue smothered by an over-doting mother. Both characters wish to be perceived as themselves and valued for themselves but this is blocked by the adults concerned. The importance of those first minutes of life is also examined, and the cruel effects of welcoming the new-born with hearty slaps. Green, it will become clear as the plays progress, has reasons why she cannot remember her early past, and the play ends with an invitation to all the audience to recall. Identity and a sense of self are informed and shaped by memory, which is, of course, a part of ourselves that dies or ceases to be when something so painful happens that it is impossible to let the experience cross the boundaries of consciousness and survive intact.

(Blue appears on stage.)

BLUE:	*(to the audience)* It all started the day we were born.
	(Green and Red appear on stage, and with Blue hold their arms across their bodies, pretending to be on the edge of giving birth. Yellow appears, the midwife. There is moaning and pushing and everyone is enjoying themselves.)
GREEN:	I can't remember being born...
BLUE:	Are you sure?
RED:	Think!
BLUE:	Think harder!
GREEN:	I told you, I don't remember!
RED:	Most people don't.
BLUE:	True.
RED:	But I do!
YELLOW:	Red's birth!
	(Green exits.)

RED: It was nice and warm in mummy's tummy. Like all babies before they come into this dangerous world, I thought I was wanted!

YELLOW: It was an easy birth.

RED: I just popped out! And looked about and everything was still. Everything was bright and cold! The first thing they did…

(Blue, as the Doctor, slaps him on the bottom. He jumps.)

Ow! …was slap my botty! I didn't cry. I –

(Red bawls.)

YELLOW: *(to the audience)* By the way, everyone, please note: when a child cries as if its heart would break, he or she really is upset.

RED: Only three minutes old, and I had learnt the world is a cruel place.

I heard my mother say:

(Green comes in as Red's Mother.)

RED'S MOTHER: Is it a girl?

(The Doctor shakes his head.)

Oh no! It's a boy. We wanted a girl. What will my husband say?

DOCTOR: He's a nice baby.

RED'S MOTHER: No, no! take it away!

(Red's Mother exits, sobbing.)

YELLOW: Meanwhile, two months later –

RED: My cousin, Blue, was born.

BLUE: I wasn't at all sure about being born. Oh dear, oh dearie me.

RED: He wasn't hit like me but kissed and hugged.

BLUE: 'Oh my precious thing!' said my mother, hugging me tight once again. Help! It was nice to be welcomed and I was glad she was pleased, but couldn't she have let go a bit? I was so very squeezed! 'Oh you'll always be mine!' she sighed. Oh dear, oh dearie me.

YELLOW:	Now you've heard about the births of Blue and Red. Red's Mum wanted a girl, and Blue's thought her boy was a toy.
RED:	I saw my mum cry.
BLUE:	I saw mine laugh. I'd been hugged.
RED:	And I'd been hit…
RED & BLUE:	But did they notice me?

(The play stops at this point. The facilitators step out from behind the stage, still holding the puppets and ask the following questions, or other questions like them.)

- What did you notice about the births of Red and Blue?
- What did Red feel when he was born?
- What did Blue feel when he was born?
- What would have made Red's birth better?
- What would have made Blue's birth better?
- Can you remember being born?
- What were you like?
- If you can't remember being born, and most people can't, what is your first memory?
- Draw a picture to do with this play or write about your own birthday.

Everything a Baby Needs

This play is clearly related to the brainstorm on what a baby, toddler and four year old need to be safe and healthy. Here the interactive work is done mid-play when the emotional situation of the characters makes them need the audience's help to suggest everything a baby needs. Although it may seem risky to rouse unfulfilled needs through this questioning and seemingly provoke an unnecessary invitation to grieve, it is only when an acknowledgement of what was lacking is made and mourned that true healing can begin, and those unmet needs have a chance at last of being met.

(Green appears.)

GREEN:	*(to the audience)* Everything a baby needs.
	(Blue and Red enter.)
	I can't remember being born…
BLUE:	Are you sure?

RED:	Think!
BLUE:	Think harder!
GREEN:	I've told you. I don't remember!
RED:	Most people don't.
BLUE:	True.
GREEN:	...but I know I had everything a baby needs. Milk.
BLUE:	Icy cold milk!
GREEN:	Love.
RED:	Love!
GREEN:	A baby needs –
BLUE:	Mashup food.
GREEN:	And to smell nice.
BLUE:	Nappies!

BLUE: *(He giggles.)*

Er!

GREEN: Toys.

BLUE: *(agreeing)* Toys.

(Green and Blue ask the audience what else they think a baby needs. Red gets very cross.)

RED: Stop it! *(loudly)* Stop it!

(Yellow appears.)

YELLOW: What is it, Red?

RED: I want them to be quiet.

YELLOW: Why?

RED: Because they got everything they needed as a baby and I didn't.

YELLOW: But it's good to know what you needed even if you never got it.

(Green and Blue nod.)

What does a baby need? What did you need?

RED:	I dunno.
GREEN:	What? Please, Red.
BLUE:	Join in.
RED:	A pram maybe.

(Blue puts his arm round Red.)

BLUE:	A friend!
RED:	Maybe.
GREEN:	Baby powder!
RED:	A mum!
BLUE:	A dad!
YELLOW:	People to love you.
RED:	Someone to cuddle you. To smell nice...no, I've just said that.
GREEN:	No, I've just said that!
RED:	Oh yeah...yeah! A tickle to make baby laugh!
YELLOW:	Yes!
RED:	Not to be bruised and beaten up.
YELLOW:	Warmth.
BLUE:	Fresh air!
RED:	Attention!
YELLOW:	Yes.
RED:	And comfort... I wish I had been comforted when I cried!

(Red starts to cry. They comfort him.)

YELLOW:	Oh Red, you knew what you needed even if you didn't get it. Good for you.
BLUE & GREEN:	Yes, good for Red! Good for you, Red!
RED:	Thank you. You've cheered me up.
BLUE:	Well, we're your friends, Red.
GREEN:	And that's what friends are for.

Blue and Green's First Birthday

Here the over-attentive mother is presented again at her son's birthday party which she responds to as if it were her own. One of the most widespread and unrecognised forms of child abuse is the child being used, before he or she can consciously and freely choose, to be the friend/companion/chaste lover of the parent or primary carer. Here the child's birthday is the pretext for the mother's unsatisfied desire for attention, which she expresses by usurping her son's celebration as if it were her own. She then goes on to have intense feelings of disappointment when her son responds differently from her own fantasy of how such a celebration should be, and she wants to hurt him, and seems only stopped by Yellow's perceptive gaze. Indeed, Yellow speaks the unarguable truth on the behalf of the innocent when she says 'however frustrated you are, and whatever they have done, hurting babies is wrong'.

(Blue and Green appear on opposite sides and come towards each other, cooing with curiosity.)

BLUE:	Green and me's first birthday.
GREEN	Blue and me met at nursery.
BLUE:	Our nursery teacher was Yellow. Green and me had the same birthday.
BLUE:	We were born on the same day.
GREEN:	I just said that.
BLUE:	*(to the audience)* Our first birthday.

(Blue and Green fall fast asleep. Yellow enters.)

YELLOW:	Fast asleep!

(They start to snore gently.)

We had to wait for them to wake up.

(They wake up and make baby noises.)

Blue's mum was there. She came to the nursery. She bought the cake. It was big and it was...

BLUE:	It was like something out of this world. But she wouldn't let us cut it and get on and eat it. She said,
GREEN:	'Make a wish, Blue, and blow the candle out,'
BLUE:	...and she hugged me and squeezed me. She was so excited. Like it was her birthday, not mine.

GREEN: 'Come on, smile, Blue and blow the candle out,'

BLUE: ...she said again. Even then I thought – 'leave it out, mother'. But I did as she wanted and Green helped me.

GREEN: We blew the candle out with one big puff. Like this. One, two, three!

(They blow the candle out.)

BLUE: Then my mum cried,

GREEN: 'Did you see that! I didn't know he could do that! What a clever good boy Blue is!'

BLUE: ...and she went to hug me but I pinched her really hard, I was so fed up.

GREEN: And then Blue's mum shouted at the top of her voice, 'Oh you nasty bad boy. You've hurt Mummy. Naughty, naughty!'

YELLOW: Blue's mum went to hit Blue. She lifted her hand to smack him really hard but she saw me looking at her and she stopped herself. She knew it was wrong because however frustrated you are, and whatever they have done, hurting babies is wrong.

GREEN: Blue's Mum looked cross but she didn't hit Blue. She just muttered under her breath, 'He started it' and went off into a corner and sulked. But I've always loved my food...

BLUE: And so have I.

GREEN: So we got stuck in.

(Blue and Green eat the cake hungrily.)

YELLOW: And they ate and they ate the delicious cake they were...

GREEN: Almost –

BLUE: But not quite –

BOTH: Sick!

- What did Blue's Mum bring to the birthday party?
- Why do you think Blue's Mum was excited?
- Why do you think she wanted to hug Blue?

- Why do you think she wanted to hit Blue?
- What would you have done if you had been Blue?
- What do you think of what Yellow said and did?
- Do you like your food?
- Can you remember your first birthday?

Blue's Cousin, Red

Here Red appears again, newly arrived at nursery school. This play shows him bullying his cousin, Blue, who after many acts of patience, punches Red back. Yellow demonstrates how to have and to feel strong feelings but not act on them, perhaps one of the most salient learning points of the whole workshop curriculum.

(Green and Blue appear.)

GREEN: Blue and me had been at nursery school for almost a year –

BLUE: When my cousin Red came onto the scene.

(Red enters, jumping up and down.)

RED: I'm Red. And I'm hyper!

(Red goes mad, screaming, jumping up and down and shaking his head. Blue and Green get out of his way and stare at him. Yellow appears.)

YELLOW: Blue, show your cousin Red around the school so that he knows where everything is.

BLUE: Yes, Miss.

(Yellow exits. Blue points at a peg and Red follows him.)

BLUE: This is my peg. That's Green's peg and that is yours.

(Red pushes Blue.)

RED: I want yours.

BLUE: No.

(Red pushes Blue again.)

BLUE: Don't.

(Blue points to the opposite side.)

That is the Babies' Room, but we don't go in there because we're the Big Children.

(Red punches him. Blue doesn't punch him back.)

BLUE: Don't.

(He moves to another part of the stage and Red follows.)

This is the big toilets and the big sinks.

(Red punches him in the stomach. Blue moves away from him.)

Don't.

(But Red punches him again and Blue now hits him back.)

RED: You peanutback!

BLUE: You carrot-walking-head.

RED: *(shouting for Yellow)* Oy lady, lady!

(Yellow appears.)

YELLOW: You both look very upset. What happened?

BLUE: He punched me. *(To Blue, outraged)* Don't punch, no. Don't punch.

(Blue goes to a corner of the stage.)

BLUE: I'm in the naughty boy's corner. I punched him in his eye 'cos he's the new boy.

YELLOW: Did you!?

(Blue bursts into tears and Red cries too.)

BLUE: You started it.

RED: No, I didn't.

BLUE: You did!

(Red and Blue fight again. Yellow separates them.)

RED: I'm lying.

YELLOW: Don't hurt each other. It makes you both angry and upset and doesn't settle anything.

RED: Hurting is wrong.

YELLOW: No punching here.

BLUE: I couldn't help it. He hit me first.

YELLOW: Nobody likes getting hurt. That's why we mustn't do it to other people. If you feel angry and...

(She acts out being in a rage, stamping and shouting and shaking her head. Red and Blue watch, fascinated.)

…you don't have to act on it. You could get hurt. And don't take it out on yourself. Don't beat yourself up or hurt yourself, if you are angry and it seems no one understands or it's not fair. Take it out on a cushion, for instance, and get it out of your system.

(She mimes punching a cushion really hard and often. Blue and Red watch and cheer.)

BLUE & GREEN: Yeah! Go for it!

(Yellow stands up, her anger spent. Blue and Red clap her demonstration.)

YELLOW: Now you two. Are you friends or what?

(They eye each other cautiously and then decide to make up. They hug each other.)

YELLOW: Great! Good for you!

BLUE & GREEN: Yes! Good for us!

Red Falls in Love

The depth and intensity of young people's feelings is often denied, especially their ability to fall in love, which they may do from an early age with another person, or pet or special object. This play explores those feelings which Red feels as well as Blue's feelings of being left out and being made invisible.

(Red and Blue enter.)

RED: Do you remember when I first met Green?

BLUE: When you first met Green? Yes, I do!

RED: It was love at first sight.

(Yellow appears.)

YELLOW: I remember too. I was getting ready to make some cakes…

RED: When Green came into the nursery.

(Green enters, unaware of Red looking at her.)

YELLOW: I saw behind me…

BLUE: Red tiptoes up and…

(Blue and Yellow see Red kissing Green shyly on her cheek.)

YELLOW: That was sweet of you, Red, to kiss Green.

(Green is embarrassed and pleased and hides her face in her hands.)

(To the audience) He turned round, looked at me and said:

RED: Green is such a love, she is.

YELLOW: He said it like an old man with dreamy eyes – really seriously.

BLUE: I was jealous. No one noticed me. I had sort of disappeared. It was like I wasn't there.

RED: It didn't last long. Next day when I saw Green I rushed up to kiss her again but she turned her face away and said:

GREEN: I don't think it's going to work. We're too young.

(Green goes off, leaving Red heartbroken.)

YELLOW: Are you all right, Red?

(Red shakes his head.)

RED: Please keep close to me.

YELLOW: And Blue – come and join me. Don't stay all alone.

BLUE: Oh! I thought you had forgotten me.

RED: I couldn't do that.

YELLOW: I never have and I never will.

(Blue joins Yellow and Red. This play can either end here or go on into the following song which is simply sung to an appropriate tune or can be spoken by the characters as a poem, shared between them, with Red taking the lead emotionally.)

The Peg Song

I'm standing where we hang our coats
And looking at your picture by the peg
Your anorak is next to another boy's hat
I wish it was by mine instead.

Noone sees me watching by the door
We're just about to have our tea
I can see you sitting by your best friend
I wish you would sit next to me.

And later on when the daylight has gone
You'll smile and hurry off home
But if someone was late
You'd have to wait
And for once we could play on our own.

So I stand where we hang our coats
And look at your picture on the wall
I don't think you know that I'm your best friend
I don't think I'm special at all.

- What did Red say happened as soon as he saw Green?
- How did what Red felt make Blue feel?
- What reason did Green give for not wanting to go ahead with the relationship Red wanted?
- Why did Blue feel no one noticed him?
- Was it true?
- What do you think she meant by that?
- How did Yellow make Red feel better?

A Very Special Tea

This is a complex play about innocence and the abuse of trust. The first half shows the Colours transforming the ordinary into magic through innocent play, being able to relate together easily and have fun, and showing the ability to imagine the future. An adult, Red's father, changes this situation suddenly by taking Red away and disguising the lack of information he gives by saying it is secret. The concept of trust is examined in the short song or poem and the play ends with a feeling of sadness at Red's mysterious absence which is finally and fully resolved in a later play, *Red's Story*.

(Green appears.)

GREEN: *(to the audience)* We were really quite old, at least four, when we had a very special tea.

             (Blue appears.)

BLUE: We made mud pies in the garden.

             (Green appears and they all run about in the garden. Yellow appears and gives them a big bowl and a wooden spoon.)

GREEN:	We got a big mixing bowl, and a wooden spoon, put in the mud, and stirred. Added a pinch of grass and this and that...

(Blue puts something wiggly into the bowl. Green takes it out.)

Urgh! No! And then we stirred, and stirred –

(Yellow takes bowl.)

YELLOW:	I'll go inside and bake it.

(Yellow goes.)

GREEN:	Meanwhile I played my favourite joke.

(They run around. Green catches Blue.)

Blue! Blue!

BLUE:	What?
GREEN:	Nuffink!

(She roars with laughter. They run around again, perhaps through the audience. She catches Red.)

GREEN:	Red!
RED:	What?
GREEN:	Nothing!

(She roars with laughter again. They begin to chase her when Yellow appears with a fruit cake. She gives each a piece of cake.)

GREEN:	Delicious.
RED:	Delicious.
BLUE:	*(to audience, rubbing his tum)* Yum! We all pretended she had made the mud pie into a cake.
YELLOW:	*(to Red)* What do you want to be when you grow up, Red?
RED:	A lawyer.
YELLOW:	You, Green?
GREEN:	Oh, something to do with food!
YELLOW:	What about you, Blue?
BLUE:	I want to be a woman.
YELLOW:	Oh?

(She accepts his ambition thoughtfully.)

Some more cake?

RED: *(to audience)* Then suddenly my father appeared. 'Daddy, what are you doing here?' I cried. I asked him if we were going somewhere. He nodded his head. 'Where are we going, daddy?' I said. He told me it was a secret. But Mum had never said anything about it. I didn't want to go.

(Red cries and stamps his feet.)

'I want more cake,' I cried. But I knew I would have to go. I got my things. 'Come on daddy, let's go,' I sighed. And I went with him.

GREEN: Goodbye, Red.

YELLOW: See you tomorrow.

BLUE: Lucky thing!

(Red moves away in slow motion, waving to his friends and Yellow while they sing this song or say its words as another kind of parting poem. Alternatively, the song-poem can be omitted and the actions cuts straight to the closing lines of the scene.)

Blues for Red

Red goes with daddy
'cause he trusts him
That is what daddies are for.
Daddy's big and strong
He'll look after him
That's what daddies are for.
But that was the last time we saw Red
And none of us knew
Where he had gone.

BLUE: That was the last time we saw Red.

YELLOW: We missed him very much.

GREEN: We missed him a lot.

BLUE: Yes, we did. And none of us knew where he had gone.

- What were Red, Green and Blue doing in the nursery garden?
- What did they pretend the mud pie had turned into?

- Have you ever pretended that something you've made changes into something else?
- What's your favourite game of tag?
- Can you remember what Red, Green and Blue want to be when they grow up?
- Do you know what you want to be when you grow up?
- Why did Red's father come to the tea party?
- When Red asked where they were going, what did his father say?
- Where do you think they were going?
- Yellow, Red and Blue never saw Red again. How did they feel?
- What could have made them feel less sad?
- Write your own poem or draw a picture about saying goodbye.
- And now write or draw a poem or picture about saying 'hello' to someone, or perhaps a pet, that you wanted to see again and say how it felt.

The Parting Poem

This play is the last presented in the *Trust And Power* workshops and appears here in a slightly changed form, with no elephant or dragon puppets. If these plays are used with participants who have completed the *Trust and Power* workshops, then this play will serve as a bridge between those sessions and these plays which reveal more of the Colours and their stories. Again, the value of the story is unchanged from the *Learning* workshop in that it shows how separation can take place without the anger of that loss destroying the significance of the relationship.

(Yellow appears.)

YELLOW: This is a story about saying goodbye. Saying goodbye can be the hardest thing in the world, but we all have to sometimes. Red, Green and Blue...

            (Presents puppets.)

            All went to the same nursery school when they were very small.

            Do you remember?

BLUE: Oh yes! That where I met the first person who I ever remember being kind and loving – Yellow.

GREEN: *(to the audience)* Yellow was our nursery school teacher.

RED: She was beautiful.

BLUE: She always had a warm smile.

RED: With which she welcomed us in the mornings.

GREEN: She used to give hugs that were really comforting.

BLUE: My thoughts about her are always dreamy.

RED: I always picture her on a sunny day.

            (Red leaves.)

BLUE: Soon after Red left the nursery –

GREEN: His father came and took him away.

BLUE: It was time for Green and I to leave too. We were old enough to go to Big School, as we called it.

GREEN: We meant primary school.

BLUE: We felt very sad saying goodbye to Yellow. It was sunny on that day.

GREEN: Which day?

YELLOW: The Colours' last day at nursery.

GREEN: Our last day at nursery.

YELLOW: Good morning. Asalaam wai alaicum. Bon jour.

GREEN: *(sadly, to Yellow)* Wai alaicum salaam.

BLUE: Bonjour, Miss. Good morning.

GREEN: We're going to miss you a lot.

YELLOW: I'll miss you too. But whenever you do, remember this: 'Whatever is in front of us –'

BLUE: 'Whatever is in front of us –'

YELLOW: 'Whatever is behind us –'

GREEN: 'Whatever is behind us –'

YELLOW: 'Is nothing compared to –'

GREEN: 'Is nothing compared to –'

YELLOW: 'What is between us.'

BLUE & GREEN: 'What is between us.'

YELLOW: Can you remember that?

BLUE: Yes.

YELLOW: That's brilliant. You are clever.

BLUE & GREEN: Bye.

> *(They hug her quickly and walk away. Yellow exits.)*

BLUE: Gone. Why am I so upset?

GREEN: You're just missing her.

BLUE: Don't tell anyone else.

GREEN: Huh?

BLUE: Don't tell anyone else.

GREEN: Right.

BLUE: Right. I hope we never have to part.

GREEN: We've always been friends. We always will be.

BLUE: Whatever is in front of us –

GREEN: Whatever is behind us is nothing –

BLUE & GREEN: Compared to what is between us.

> *(Yellow appears.)*

YELLOW: Although they grew up and many things happened to them,
            they did never forget me, and I never forgot them. I always
            thought of the Parting Poem. 'Whatever is in front of us –'

BLUE & GREEN: *(encouraging the audience to join in)* 'Whatever is in front of
            us –'

YELLOW: 'Whatever is behind us –'

EVERYONE: 'Whatever is behind us –'

YELLOW: 'Is nothing compared to –'

EVERYONE: 'Is nothing compared to –'

YELLOW: 'What is between us.'

EVERYONE: 'What is between us.'

YELLOW:	*(to the audience)* Thank you for joining in!
GREEN:	*(to the audience)* You are clever!
BLUE:	Good for you!
GREEN:	And good for us all!

- Can you remember leaving a place or a person?
- How did you feel?
- Did you go to a play school or nursery school?
- Do you remember anything about it?
- Write your own parting poem or draw a picture about saying goodbye.

Blue's Story

Informed by the story *Mrs. Alvarez* from the first workshop *Trust*, this play is longer than any that have gone before, and with *Red's Story* and *Green's Story*, examines in depth some of the most serious affronts so far to self-esteem and protection issues. In it the consequences of low expectations are exposed, and the so-called chain of abuse. Mrs. Alvarez here becomes Mrs. Tangerine, a pedagogue who stands in opposition to the advocacy of Yellow. Young people very often do not understand the tones of irony or sarcasm or their inverted meaning, taking words at their face value. This is Blue's case whose innocence is rewarded with physical punishment as Mrs. Tangerine metes out to others, supposedly in her care, the treatment she experienced herself when young as a way of denying its pain. As well as Mrs. Tangerine's negative expectations of Blue, negative naming is also examined, developing the theme of naming which is of key importance throughout both the *Trust And Power* workshops as well as in these additional stories and plays. In this play, Blue is still his mother's care-taker in a distortion of the parent-child relationship, and his own individuality still smothered. It is only when his mother wants to take his photograph that he rebels and asserts his own identity and, with effort and courage, revives his ambitions and expectations of and for himself, witnessed by Yellow. She leads the congratulations and at the last, Blue can accept the applause of the audience with neither apology nor arrogance.

(Blue appears with Green.)

BLUE: Green and me –

(Mrs. Tangerine, played by Red, appears and interrupts him.)

MRS. TANGERINE: 'Green and I', boy! 'Green and I!' Do at least try to be grammatically correct!

(Blue sighs.)

BLUE: Green and I looked forward to going to the big school and it was great when we got there –

GREEN: Some days I thought, 'I am so happy I'm going to burst'.

BLUE: *(sadly)* I remember but –

GREEN: I was quick.

BLUE: I was slow.

GREEN: I was bright.

BLUE: But I was dim. I'll tell you how dim I was. I was so dim I didn't realise I was stupid until I was eight years old!

GREEN: *(moving away from him)* I went up into a different class from Blue.

(She goes, waving to Blue.)

Goodbye, Blue. See you after school!

BLUE: Bye.

(He picks up a book and tries to read.)

It was hard for me to read and spell. My mum bought me books and then when I couldn't read them easily, she gave them all away. I soon hated school and dreaded going in.

(He walks reluctantly as if to school and picks up a book and struggles to read it. Yellow appears to narrate the story.)

YELLOW: One day, Blue was sitting in the classroom by the window. It was very hot, the sun was pouring in. He felt so sleepy he closed his eyes and he didn't see Mrs. Tangerine, his teacher, coming over to him.

(Mrs. Tangerine appears and goes over to Blue.)

MRS. TANGERINE: Blue!

(He starts and opens his eyes. Mrs. Tangerine points to the book.)

Read this.

(Blue struggles.)

Well?

(Blue is silent.)

(sarcastically) You look sleepy. Do you want to go home, Blue?

YELLOW: Blue didn't realise that Mrs. Tangerine was being sarcastic and didn't mean what she said. He thought 'That's the first sensible thing anyone's said all day!'

BLUE: Yes, Mrs. Tangerine, can I?

YELLOW: And then Mrs. Tangerine hit him round the head.

MRS. TANGERINE: Honestly, boy, you've half a brain.

YELLOW: It is against the law for teachers to hit pupils.

MRS. TANGERINE: It was for his own good.

YELLOW: How could it be? If we hit our children, all they learn is to hit.

If we frighten our children all they learn is fear.

BLUE: I felt small. I thought I was being punished for being thick. I was so angry.

YELLOW: People with power over young people should look after them and not abuse their trust.

MRS. TANGERINE: Well! I was slapped when I was a child and look at me. It never did me any harm!

(She goes off angrily. Yellow exits in the opposite direction.)

BLUE: But the new name stuck. Wherever I went in the school, in the playground, in the corridor, I heard the others chanting 'Half-a-Brain! Half-a-Brain!' By now, I didn't just hate school, I hated myself. But that was then and this is now! Watch this space!

(Blue goes to one side of the stage to present the next part of his story.)

Can Half-a-Brain who's meant to fail win through in the end?

It all started on my eleventh birthday. Mum was giving me a surprise party but I had to pretend I didn't know. After school, I made myself go home. I made myself look happy. I made myself ready to be surprised. I took a deep breath and opened the door. There was my Mum in a party hat.

(Blue's Mum appears, played by Red.)

BLUE'S MUM: Surprise! Surprise!

BLUE: *(pretending to be surprised)* Oh!

BLUE'S MUM: *(singing)* 'Happy birthday to you, happy birthday to you....'

(She gives him a birthday cake with candles.)

BLUE'S MUM: I remember your first birthday. You blew the candle out all by yourself.

BLUE: I did not.

BLUE'S MUM: You did.

BLUE: No, you did.

BLUE'S MUM: Don't argue with me on your birthday, darling, I'm tired and emotional!

(She cries.)

BLUE: Oh, Mum.

(He sighs.)

What game would you like to play?

BLUE'S MUM: Look what I've got you for your birthday.

(She opens her present to him.)

A camera.

(She shows it to him.)

BLUE: Thank you. Just what you've always wanted!

BLUE'S MUM: *(with the camera ready)* Smile, darling! Smile for Mummy!

BLUE: *(to the audience)* Smile! I wanted to cry! That's when I thought 'Enough's enough! I've been pushed around for too long.' I said to Mum...

(He turns to his mother.)

I don't want my photo taken now, but thank you very much for the camera. I'm going to my room.

BLUE'S MUM: But why, darling? It's your birthday. I've got some lovely games for us to play. Don't spoil the day for me.

BLUE: I'm going to my room to write.

BLUE'S MUM: Write! But you can't even read!

BLUE: Maybe, but who knows? I might surprise all of you. No one believes what I say so I'm going to try and write the truth down!

(Blue's Mum goes off without another word.)

BLUE: I started my story. I wrote it all down. Everything that I thought and felt and wanted. And something changed. It was me. I stopped believing I had half a brain.

(Yellow appears, applauding.)

YELLOW: Good for you!

BLUE: Thank you. I did surprise them all in the end. So you see, you can write if you have something to say!

- Do you remember your first day in 'Big School'? If so, write or draw a picture about it.
- Green was told she was bright and quick. What was Blue told he was?
- Why did Mrs. Tangerine hit Blue?
- What did she call him?
- How do you think Blue felt when people called him 'Half-a-Brain'?
- How old was Blue when his mother gave him a camera for his birthday?
- Why do you think he didn't want his Mum to take his photo?
- Why did Blue want to write down his story?
- Have you ever been told you can't do something and then you have?
- Write about or draw a picture of something you thought you could never do.

Red's Story

This play, which resolves what happens to Red after *A Very Special Tea*, is presented multilingually in Bengali, (Ben) and in a dialect of Bengali, Sylheti, (Syl) both of which are written phonetically, and in British Sign Language (BSL) with its signs written as words in the order of that language's syntax. As each language has its own perceived status and power which changes according to context and place, so it can be in a multilingual structure that different languages are used to further particular strands of communication. For instance, here, English tends to be the language of information and sometimes of dominance, whilst Bengali and Sylheti Bengali are the language of longing and BSL of action and emotion. It must be remembered that using an expressive and gestural language like British Sign Language adds immeasurably to the dramatic action of the play as it reveals meaning through physicality and happens in the emotional present. This play, of course, can be adapted monolingually and is also given here as an example of possible multilingual structures.

This is a story of migration and dispossession and of well-intentioned adults causing hurt by withholding information and by doing what they think to be best without finding out if it is. Because children's literal survival depends on the care they receive, Red protects his parents from his own anger and feels he must be to blame for the hurt he suffers. Because the story and its flashback narrative devices are quite sophisticated, any follow-up work or discussion need only be brief, unless they are to be extended into another session. Don't be put off by this play's multilingual presentation which looks far more complicated on paper than it does on stage. It, like all the others, can be adapted as necessary.

(Red appears.)

RED:	*(to the audience in BSL)* Blue. Red. Yellow. Forget them never. Like picture, my mind. *(Eng)* That's where I had a good time, at Nursery. I bullied them all but they still liked me! My last day in Nursery School. *(BSL)* Play, Red, Blue, run.

(He runs and Green and Blue run on to join him. Yellow enters with the cake and they gather round her excitedly.)

RED:	*(to the audience, Syl)* Kintho forey...

(He turns as if to look at his father appearing.)

...dekhi amar abba aichon. *(Eng)* Daddy!

YELLOW:	*(BSL)* Mr. Red.
GREEN:	*(Eng)* Have some cake.
BLUE:	*(Ben)* Cake chai?
RED:	*(Syl)* Abba afney kitha korai? *(to the audience; Eng)* I asked him if we were going somewhere. *(Syl)* Amra koi jairam abba? *(BSL)* Where? Told me secret. *(Eng)* But Mum had never said. *(Syl)* Ami aro cake kaitham.

(Red cries and stamps his feet.)

(Syl) Ami aro cake kaitham. *(Eng)* But I knew I would have to go.

	(Syl) Cholo abba jaigi. *(Eng)* And I went with him.
YELLOW:	*(Eng)* Goodbye, Red.
GREEN:	*(BSL)* See you tomorrow.
BLUE:	*(BSL)* Lucky you.
YELLOW:	*(BSL)* Red go Daddy. Trust him. Daddy big, strong. Will care Red. Daddies do.
GREEN:	*(Eng)* Red went with Daddy 'cos he trusted him. Daddy's big and strong He'd look after Red. That's what daddies are for.
YELLOW:	Aeroplane. Fly.

(Red is centre stage as his story is told.)

BLUE:	*(Ben)* Amra khob kooshi korsi. Ammarey rakhia gesoin.
GREEN:	*(BSL)* Mummy gone.
YELLOW:	*(Eng)* Mummy is left behind. But that's okay –

(Red smiles.)

(BSL) Because Mummy trusts Daddy…

BLUE	*(Ben)* Ar than abba thanrey dekhba.
YELLOW:	*(Eng)* He takes Red to this new place where everything is warm and loving and caring.
RED:	*(BSL)* All warm, loving, caring.
BLUE:	*(Ben)* Noia jagath khoob schoondor ar aran asil. Lal kooshi asla kinthu aktook dhoroi asoon.
RED:	*(Syl)* Amma koi? *(Eng)* Why hasn't Mummy come? Doesn't she love me any more?
GREEN:	*(BSL)* Daddy say will get Mummy.
YELLOW:	Daddy says he will go and get Mummy.
BLUE:	*(Ben)* Ar Red kooshi asun.

(Red smiles.)

(Eng) I'll go with you. No? *(Syl)* Acha abba thumi ammarey gia anno. *(BSL)* Quick, please. Want Mummy want.

(Red waves goodbye.)

RED: *(Eng)* My father didn't come back. Not for a year and a day.

GREEN: *(BSL)* Father no come. Wait one year, one day.

RED: *(Syl)* Ammar abba ar feria aisoon nai. Ami boochinai khenai amar abba ammarai loiya feria aisoon nai.

GREEN: Red think punishment, bad. Parents not love. Only four.

RED: *(Eng)* I thought I had done something wrong. That's why they didn't love me. I was only four. *(Syl)* Amar boish matro char asil. Ami mono khorsi ami soitani khori. El laggi ararey bhal fey nai.

YELLOW: *(Eng)* They thought he'd be happy.

GREEN: *(BSL)* They thought forget, Red happy. Poor, couldn't care probably Red but not tell Red what do.

BLUE: *(Eng)* They thought they were too poor to take care of Red properly. They didn't tell him what they were going to do, they thought he was too young to understand.

RED: *(Syl)* Amarey kichoo koisen na kitha khorben. Monokhorso ami khoob shoto. Ita bhoostam nai. *(Eng)* While I was away, they had another child, a little girl.

YELLOW: *(BSL)* Red away, Mum Dad another baby, girl. Always wanted girl.

RED: *(Syl)* Ami ono thaktey amar ar shoto bhon oisey. *(Eng)* The daughter they had always wanted. It has taken me a long time to learn to trust again, to let myself look forward to the future.

BLUE: *(BSL)* Red trust again long time have. Now look future.

RED: *(Syl)* Ami achon amar bhonrey khoob bhala fai.

GREEN: *(BSL)* Now baby sister loves loves.

RED: *(Eng)* And to love my sister. Which I do. Very much.

(Yellow, Blue and Green cheer Red.)

ALL: Good for you!

- What happened in this story?
- What do you think of what Red's father did?

- Do you think he could have done something different?
- Why did it take Red some time to love his little sister?
- Have you ever been on a long journey? If you have, write about it or draw a picture. If you haven't, where would you like to go? Write about where you would like to go or draw a picture.

Green's Story

This play deals directly with the sexual abuse of a young girl and its consequences for their family. Green is left vulnerable after her father's death. When her mother remarries, her stepfather, White, starts to come into her room. Without being coy, the play includes enough information to be clear about Green's plight without causing anxiety or distress to its audience. Dealing with strong emotions, the play looks at the value of friendship in the face of grief, fear and sexual abuse and at the role of the advocate, someone who is on your side and speaks for you if you want them to. Green describes how she was changed by her experience, exhibiting many of the signs of an abused person, such as sleeplessness, self-neglect, weight loss, disruptive and hurtful behaviour and lack of trust but how too, finally, she has learnt to accept herself and what has happened to her whilst still wondering how her life might have been if things had been different.

(Green appears with a pencil and book.)

GREEN: Although we were in different classes, Blue and me –

(She corrects herself hastily.)

Blue and I were still friends.

(She reads from her book.)

'My Summer Holidays'. On my summer holidays I went camping with my friend Blue in an orchard. His mum stayed in the big house. The food was lovely and you could get as much as you wanted but I had to come home early because my Dad was killed by a car.

(She looks up.)

It wasn't his fault but I felt –

(She throws the exercise book to the floor.)

I still loved school.

(She picks her book up.)

I was doing well. And it got me out of the house. But getting there…there was the road!

(She freezes.)

(Yellow appears.)

YELLOW: She wanted to cross, but she was frightened if she did, big cars would come and open their bonnets and teeth would grow and eat her up.

(Green covers her face in fear. Blue appears.)

BLUE: Green, Green!

GREEN: What? What is it?

BLUE: Nuffink! And nothing to be afraid of.

GREEN: He took my hand and…

(She hesitates. He smiles. He takes her hand and they cross the road, looking left and right.)

YELLOW: …they crossed the road.

GREEN: Blue got me through. He was always there for me when I needed him.

YELLOW: Things got better.

GREEN: They had to. Mum even married again. Then, when I was ten, Something Happened I couldn't tell anyone about, although I tried.

Blue! Blue!

BLUE: What?

(She pauses.)

GREEN: Nothing.

(She imitates his expression.)

Don't look so worried.

(She walks off.)

BLUE: It was like Green was only pretending to still be friends. She was always tired and had no time for me. Shortly before our eleventh birthday, I went round her house.

(Blue mimes throwing little stones against her window to attract her attention. Green appears.)

GREEN: What do you want?

BLUE: It's our birthday soon. What are we going to do?

GREEN: Your mother's having a surprise party for you.

(Blue is surprised. Green mocks him.)

Ah! Didn't you know?

BLUE: No.

GREEN: And surprise, surprise. I'm not going to be there.

BLUE: What's wrong?

GREEN: Nothing. Okay?

BLUE: 'Whatever is in front of us...'

GREEN: Oh please!

BLUE: You've changed.

GREEN: Then go and find someone else to be friends with.

(She disappears.)

BLUE: Green! (To the audience) I blamed myself although I didn't know what I had done wrong.

(He goes off as Green re-appears.)

GREEN: I wanted him to know but I didn't want to have to tell him. Then I thought, okay, I'll keep all my secrets to myself.

YELLOW: Green felt that all her happy times had been a trick.

(Green looks at her.)

You don't have to say. Not if you don't want to.

GREEN: No. This is my story –

YELLOW: I'm here, if you need me.

(Green takes a deep breath.)

GREEN: – and I am going to tell it. The worst day of my life and my Mother's was the day White, my step-father, came into our house.

It was like he was made of glass and if we didn't do exactly what he said he'd explode and cut us all to pieces. When I was ten, he started coming into my room at nights. He'd tried to get close to me and kiss me. I was terrified.

YELLOW: He said, 'If you tell anyone, you'll never see your Mum again.'

GREEN: I didn't know what to do. Life became unbearable. I thought if I don't tell I'll burst. I decided to tell a teacher, but he didn't listen. My teacher always seemed so far away.

YELLOW: She tried to tell Blue.

GREEN: Blue! Blue!

(Blue appears.)

BLUE: What?

GREEN: Nothing.

BLUE: I didn't know what to do. I couldn't get through to her.

GREEN: I felt dirty and alone in the world. On the outside I was still cheerful. No one could guess at the mess I was inside. I stopped eating. No one noticed. No one noticed me. But then I remembered – Yellow. I went back to Nursery School and they told me where she was. I found her and told her. She believed me. I laughed with relief. She thanked me for telling her and said it wasn't my fault.

YELLOW: I talked to Green's Mum and we went to the Police.

GREEN: When questioned, White said I was wicked and wanted attention.

YELLOW: The police believed Green but they didn't have enough evidence to convict White. Green and her mother left home and stayed with some friends.

GREEN: We were lucky. We never saw White again.

(She comes down to the audience.)

I can't change what's happened to me or to you and I often wonder how things might have been. It's taken me time not to feel ashamed of my past, but it's not too late. And at last I can say: I would never have chosen this path, but I am very glad to be who I am, where I am now.

YELLOW & BLUE: **Good for you!**

(Green goes to her friends and hugs them.)

GREEN: And you! Thank you, Yellow! Thank you, Blue!

- Blue is Green's friend because he has always been there for her. What do you think makes a good friend?
- When Green threw her book on the ground, what do you think she was feeling?
- Why was Green afraid of crossing the road?
- What was the worst day of Green's life?
- Why couldn't Green talk to anyone about what was happening to her?
- Why was it so important to Green that Yellow believed her?
- What happened to her step-father, White?
- At the end of the play, why does Green say 'I am very glad to be who I am where I am now'?
- What do you like most about Green?
- Write about or draw a picture of Green.

Epilogue

This short epilogue can be used, like the *Prologue,* for all the plays. It is presented here both monolingually and multilingually. Just as it is important to close the workshops with a debriefing section, so it is important to present the plays with a clear ending. It will be a question of choice whether to use this epilogue or whether the play or plays will be finished in another way; or whether this epilogue closes a play after its follow-up questions or discussion or whether they come after it. In any event, clapping and cheering, music and song are a positive way of bringing the attention of the audience back to reality without negating the effects of the short play or plays they have been watching.

YELLOW: This is the end of our play but not the end of our story.

GREEN: Things haven't always been great for us.

RED: But we hope they are for you.

GREEN: There's one thing remaining that we want to do –

BLUE: –– and that is to cheer all of you.

(They face the audience and cheer three times.)

Epilogue – In Three Languages

YELLOW: *(A)* This is the end of our play but not the end of our story.

GREEN: *(B)* This is not the end of our story. *(C)* Things haven't always been great for us.

RED: *(A)* But we hope they are for you.

BLUE: *(C)* But we hope they are for you.

GREEN: *(B)* There's one thing remaining that we want to do –

BLUE: *(A)* – and that is to cheer all of you.

(They face the audience and cheer three times.)

APPENDIX 1

The Original Curriculum for the Trust and Power Workshops

This is the original curriculum for six sessions around trust and power with groups of primary school students, aged between eight and nine in their fourth year of study, each involving games, exercises, stories, and short puppet plays on the theme of the workshop which formed the basis for the workshops in this book.

Theme	Basis	Content
1. Trust	games/ group	creating a safe space, listening, trust and esteem-building
2. Power	role-play	empowerment and growth, responsibility for actions
3. Body	exercise	owning feelings, difficult emotions, feeling to expression…
4. Feelings	painting	naming of feelings, expressing, asserting, communicating
5. Communicating	story	communicating feelings and memories, writing and telling a story, listening
6. Learning	problem-solving	changing a situation, self-esteem, responsibility of teachers and school

Curriculum learning goals

Session One: Trust

Knowledge

Participants learn:

- Identification and acknowledgement of messages that make you feel good from the components of trust, for example: knowing people well, feeling comfortable with people, learning from past experience.
- How to recognise when trust is being broken.
- That trust is 'built', and that the breaking of it is serious.
- How to enjoy the mutual duties and rewards of friendship.

Skills

Participants learn how to:

- Listen with increasing span of attention to other children and adults.
- Ask and respond to questions and comment on what has been said.
- Be confident in using their own first language.
- Identify and express feelings.
- Work in pairs and groups.
- Distinguish between 'positive' and 'negative' messages.
- Interpret.
- Problem-solve (e.g. by critical reflection, hypothesising, predicting, providing alternative solutions).
- Use drama skills (e.g. mime, assuming roles and working within them).
- Attitudes.
- Trust of the team and find the classroom a safe space for the work.
- Responsibility for themselves and towards classmates.

Curriculum learning goals

Session Two: Power

Knowledge

Participants learn that:

- There is a range of family and extended family roles. (They look at concepts of the life cycle, generational roles, siblings etc., and roles of carers, and different levels of caring).
- Power can be used for good or ill.
- We can ask the questions: What is power? (powerfulness) What is responsibility? (carefulness). What is the connection between the two?
- Only certain (e.g. age-related) things should be demanded of children.
- It might be necessary to run away from danger.

Skills

Participants learn how to:

- Take and give instructions.
- Complete a questionnaire.
- Measure physical strength.
- Distinguish between 'inner' and 'outer' strength.
- Role play animals and different family members.
- Interpret behaviour in stories and role play.
- Find ways to say 'no'. Find ways of getting help.
- Use a time line.
- Demonstrate responsible behaviour.

Attitudes

Participants develop:

- Confidence in relation to people with more power than they (children) have.
- Confidence with their own power and with growth in power.
- Sensitive use of power.

Curriculum learning goals

Session Three: Body

Knowledge

Participants learn:

- To recognise that their body has a 'safe' space, and to identify how large or small that is.
- The functions of the senses and parts of the body.
- The concepts of stress and relaxation (mental and physical).
- That some of their body is private and they have the right not to let people touch it.

Skills

Participants learn how to:

- Recognise and express feelings, sensations.
- Distinguish between 'good' (comfortable) and 'bad' (uncomfortable) touches.
- Identify body parts – writing, using data, diagrams, charts, drawing.
- Give a 'good' touch.
- Respond appropriately to danger (e.g. shouting, disobeying a rule etc.)

Attitudes

Participants develop:

- Esteem and care for their own bodies and respect and esteem for others.
- Awareness that each person's body is his/her own.
- Confidence that if they are in danger with an adult it is OK to shout, say no and so forth.

Curriculum learning goals

Session Four: Feelings

Knowledge

Participants learn that:

- Everyone has feelings.
- Feelings are neither good nor bad.
- They have a right to their feelings.
- They can understanding the distinction between feeling and action (e.g. anger versus violence).
- They can choose who they share their feelings with.
- Feelings give them important information about people and things (e.g. danger, love).

Skills

Participants learn how to:

- Name feelings.
- Recognise feelings in self and others (e.g. facial expression, language, body, movements, sign names).
- Express feelings: vocabulary, appropriate language for context.
- Share.
- Express feelings in drawings, poems, letters, cartoons.
- Make craftwork related to role-play and reading.
- Insert dialogue into a situation (cartoon, role-play): discuss what someone might say.

Attitudes

Participants develop awareness that:

- Feelings are important and inevitable.
- What they do with them affects other people.
- Feelings are to be trusted.
- Communicating their feelings to someone they trust can be better for them than keeping them to themselves.
- No one can take your feelings away from you, tell you that your feeling doesn't exist or doesn't matter.
- Friends and people they trust should listen to their feelings.
- Feelings make each person whole and healthy.

Curriculum learning goals

Session Five: Communicating

Knowledge

Participants learn:

- Awareness of listening skills: eye-contact, attention.
- The difference between a surprise secret and an unwelcome secret imposed on you.
- The purpose of a diary, record, letter, remembering.

Skills

Participants learn how to:

- Listen.
- Communicate a story orally: emphasise important parts, sequence and so forth.
- Participate in a group, making a story with words and illustrations.
- Talk about their own feelings with confidence.
- Assume a role in enacting scene (with puppets).
- Read aloud with expression.
- Make deductions and predictions about a story.

Attitudes

Participants develop awareness that:

- Being believed is related to past quality of communication.
- Sharing with friends and so forth means having someone to tell things to (and *vice versa*).
- Communicating is about more than just language, but that language (voice, writing, Sign) helps.
- Good communication requires trust.

Curriculum learning goals

Session Six: Learning

Knowledge

Participants learn that:

- Problems can be solved with the appropriate help.
- The can find out who to go to for advice/help.
- Making a mistake can be OK, and can help you next time.
- Trying to do something difficult risks not being able to do so.
- A positive approach to experience, success and failure, is a way to learn and gain confidence.

Skills

Participants learn how to:

- Know and ask for what they need to change a situation.
- Recognise a problem they can't solve on their own.
- Role play dilemmas in groups and pairs.
- Ask 'What if...?' questions, and answer them.
- Weigh up the risks of two courses of action and express a preference.
- Use material from all sessions in inquiry into health and safety in school/home.
- Use personal records (pictures, writings, models etc.) to make a personal response/story/poem.

Attitudes

Participants develop:

- Flexibility in problem-solving and asking for help.
- Awareness that the school has a responsibility to esteem, respect, believe, listen to pupils.
- Belief in their rights to safety, respect, being believed by teachers, carers, adults.
- A 'learning from experience' attitude.

APPENDIX 2

Useful Addresses and Telephone Numbers

Barnardo's
Head Office
Tanner's Lane
Barkingside
Ilford
Essex 1G6 1QG
Tel: 0181 550 882

British Association for Counselling (BAC)
1 Regent Place
Rugby
Warwickshire CV12 2BH
Tel: 01788 578 328

ChildLine
2nd Floor
Royal Mail Building
50 Studd Street
London N1 0QW
Tel: 0171 239 1000
Helpline, voice and minicom: 0800 1111

Childwatch
206 Hessle Road
Hull
N. Humberside HU3 3BE
Tel: 01482 25552

Children's Legal Centre
20 Compton Terrace
London N1 2UN
Tel: 0171 359 6251

The Children's Society
Edward Rudolf House
Margery Street
London WC1X OJL
Tel: 0171 837 4299

Kidscape
152 Buckingham Palace Road
London SW1W 9TR
Tel: 0171 730 3300

National Association for Pastoral Care in Education
Institute of Education
University of Warwick
Coventry CV4 7AL
Tel: 01203 523 810

National Association of Young People's Counselling and Advisory Services
(send SAE for local details to)
NAYPCAS
Magazine Business House
11 Newarke St
Leicester LE1 5SF

National Society for the Prevention of Cruelty to Children
NSPCC National Centre
42 Curtain Road
London EC2A 3NH
Child Protection Helpline (24 hour service, free call): 0800 800 500
Parentsline: 01268 757 077

The Samaritans
Head Office
10 The Grove
Slough
Berkshire SL1 1QP
Emergency 24 hour Linkline: 0345 909 090

APPENDIX 3

Suggested Puppet Design

Bibliography

Non-fiction

For adults

Bray, M. (1997) *Sexual Abuse: The Child's Voice*, London: Jessica Kingsley Publishers

Bryant-M, K. (1993) *Child Abuse*, Hove: Wayland

Griffin, S. *Pornography And Silence*, London: Women's Press

Kübler-Ross, E. (1983) *On Children and Death*, Basingstoke: Macmillan

Maher, P. (1990) 'Child Protection – Another View', *Pastoral Care*

Melzak, S. (1992) *Integrating Refugee Children Into Schools*, London: Minority Rights Groups and Medical Foundation for the Care of the Tortured

Miller, A. (1987) *The Drama of Being a Child*, London: Virago

Miller, A. (1988) *For Your Own Good*, London: Virago

Miller, A. (1991) *Thou Shalt Not Be Aware*, Harmondsworth: Penguin

For young people

Bain, O. and Sanders, M (1990) *Out In The Open*, London: Virago

Courtney, C. (1990) *Morphine and Dolly Mixtures*, Harmondsworth: Penguin

Elliot, M. (1988) *Keeping Safe*, London: New English Library

Hassell, J. (1989) *Nobody's Perfect*, London: Hutchinson

Pearce, J. (1989) *Worries and Fears*, London: Thorsons (Harper Collins)

Rouf, K. and Rouf, C. (1991) *Black Girls Speak Out*, London: Children's Society

Stones, R. (1993) *Don't Pick On Me*, London: Piccadilly Press

Fiction

For adults

Angelou, M. *I Know Why The Caged Bird Sings*, London: Virago

For young people

Chick, S. (1987) *Push Me, Pull Me*, Livewire, London: Women's Press

Hessell, J. (1987) *I'm Glad I Told Mum*, London: Beaver Books

Howard, E. (1987) *Gillyflower*, London: Collins,

Little, J. (1984) *Mama's Going To Buy You A Mocking Bird*, Harmondsworth: Puffin

Watcher, O. (1989) *Close To Home*, Harmondsworth: Viking Kestrel

Watcher, O. (1991) *No More Secrets For Me*, Harmondsworth: Viking Kestrel

Resources

Casdagli, P. (1994) *Grief, Bereavement and Change: A Drama Resource Book*, London: Daniels Publishing

Casdagli, P (1994) *The Quick Guide to Grief, Bereavement and Change*, London: Daniels Publishing

Casdagli, P. (1995) *Anti-Bullying: A Drama Resource*, London: Daniels Publishing

Index of Workshop Contents